Never Be Lonely Again

Never Be Lonely Again

THE WAY OUT OF EMPTINESS, ISOLATION, AND A LIFE UNFULFILLED

Pat Love, Ed.D., and
Jon Carlson, Psy.D., Ed.D.

Health Communications, Inc.
Deerfield Beach, Florida

www.hcibooks.com

Library of Congress Cataloging-in-Publication Data

Love, Patricia.
    Never be lonely again : the way out of emptiness, isolation, and a life unfulfilled
/ Pat Love and Jon Carlson.
        p. cm.
    Includes bibliographical references and index.
    ISBN-13: 978-0-7573-1565-7
    ISBN-10: 0-7573-1565-8
    1. Loneliness 2. Self-realization. 3. Satisfaction. 4. Loneliness—Religious
aspects—Buddhism. I. Carlson, Jon. II. Title.

    BF575.L7L68 2011
    158.2—dc22

                                                              2010048998

Publisher: Health Communications, Inc.
            3201 S.W. 15th Street
            Deerfield Beach, FL 33442–8190

Jon Carlson's back cover photo used with permission by Governor's State University
Pat Love's back cover photo used with permission by Dinkins/DeJong
Cover design by Larissa Hise Henoch
Interior design and formatting by Lawna Patterson Oldfield

To all the lonely people

Together we dedicate this book to
Jhampa Shaneman who made this journey,
this book, this blessing,
happen in our lives.

Pat dedicates this book to
the Girlfriends who pulled her away
from loneliness many years ago
and have never let go.

Jon dedicates this book to
Laura and Our Family

Contents

Part Three: **Leaving Loneliness Behind**

Exercises

Acknowledgments

We both thank our many professional and personal friends and teachers. We have deepened our respect and appreciation for our relationships through completing this project.

We want to thank our traveling companions especially Addison, Daniel, Larry, and Matt for their support, understanding, and compassion.

Our gratitude and respect remain for our special Buddhist teachers Jhampa Shaneman from Mexico, His Holiness the Dalai Lama in India, and Dr. Tipawadee Emavardhana from Bangkok, Thailand. We are also indebted to those who have taught us via their books and workshops including Jon Kabat-Zinn, Jack Kornfield, Thich Nhat Hahn, Matthieu Ricard, Philip Moffitt, Pema Chodron, and the presence that shines in the hearts of so many others.

We wish to acknowledge Steven Stosny for helping us see the importance of core values and to Alfred Adler for insights that are present throughout this text.

Our editor, Michele Matrisciani has been a fully vested partner in this project. She steered, wrangled, and pulled a book out of us, all while completing her own project, the birth of her son, Julian Joseph Rottino, born Monday, September 13, 2010. It has been our pleasure to know and work with this remarkable person and the HCI family.

Additionally, Jon wants to thanks his colleagues at Governors State University and his friend Tom Effenheim for encouragement and supply of lovingly created pens. He also wants to thank his family, especially Kirstin, Chris, and Matt, for carefully reading the various incarnations of this book, and Laura for her wisdom, support, understanding, and tolerance.

Pat wants to thank Larry Parks for not only his reading and editing but for bringing coffee at the wee hours of the morning when it was sorely needed.

Introduction

L oneliness affects all of us at different times, for different reasons, and to different degrees. For the most part, when we are lonely, we look just like ordinary people going about our lives: we go to work, tend to business, make plans, and follow through. It's our internal world that differs: we feel isolated, distant, and removed from others. Sometimes we feel empty or dead inside and out of sync with the rest of the world, as though we don't belong or something is wrong with us. We long to make a connection, but most of the time it appears just out of reach.

Loneliness consumes a significant portion of our emotional energy. Managing it, avoiding it, and dreading it become part of our personal routine, and over time, coping becomes part of the duress. Sometimes we can distract ourselves with a job or a task, but the loneliness eventually returns. Each day we harbor a small bit of hope for permanent relief from the burden of feeling lonely.

Imagine a condition so powerful and so enigmatic that two licensed therapists wouldn't talk about it or even relate it to their own lives. This was our situation. Loneliness affected us, but like many people who are lonely, we didn't fully acknowledge it. The realization that our busy and seemingly fulfilling lives were masking our internal feelings of loneliness came in the most unlikely place: India.

When we set off on our trip five years ago, we looked like two ordinary tourists. Pat is a high-energy, charismatic person. She is in demand as a professional speaker and a consultant on relationships and sexuality. She is captivating with her red hair, her smile, and her self-effacing humor. Pat is highly intelligent and has the gift of being able to make the complex simple. She maintains a private consultation practice in Austin, Texas, where she lives with her husband, Larry, and is surrounded by friends and family.

Jon is a college professor and a practicing psychologist. He and his wife, Laura, have five children and several grandchildren. They live in Lake Geneva, Wisconsin, where Jon spent his boyhood. He has written about a wide range of subjects and has created 250 professional therapy videos. Jon has traveled extensively throughout Asia, including working in Thailand yearly for more than a decade.

When we made plans to go to India, we thought of the trip mostly as a professional endeavor, but both of us secretly carried a small bit of hope that this venture would somehow break the spell of our loneliness. Neither of us spoke about this until years after the trip had ended, but in India the spell did unexpectedly break for us, individually and anonymously; when we returned home, the small bit of hope expanded into happiness, and a clear path away from loneliness was revealed. Here's how it happened.

We left for India from the central time zone, but Jon headed west (Los Angeles, Bangkok, New Delhi) and Pat went east (Atlanta, Paris, New Delhi). Jon—a tall, handsome, highly observant guy—is rather quiet, with the aura of a wise man. Pat's aura is different. She's more likely to be mistaken for the girl next door than a wise woman. Though observant in her own way, details are not her strong suit, unless they are related to a good laugh or a good time. Knowing this, Jon didn't even question why Pat traveled east while he traveled west; our twenty-five-year acquaintance had taught him that she would always show up, but in her own unique way.

Pat had learned from her long association with Jon that when he extends an invitation, you jump at it. His invitations always lead to adventures. This particular invitation just happened to include a private audience with His Holiness the Dalai Lama, so Pat said yes immediately; no details were needed. Jon's invitations were always rich with possibility, but this time neither of us had any idea how life changing this particular experience was going to be. Although the stated purpose of the trip was professional, the outcome would be far more personal than either of us could have imagined.

In the ensuing weeks, months, and years, the experiences we shared in India—marked by laughter, tears, ecstasy, and connection—transformed our lives and subsequently affected our families, our friends, and anyone who was willing to be influenced by our story.

Why India?

Jon is the quintessential networker. If we all have six degrees of separation from others in this world, Jon has only three. He is probably only two degrees away from Kevin Bacon. This knack for networking led him to a former ordained Buddhist monk, Jhampa Shaneman, who for several years studied in residence with His Holiness the Dalai Lama. Jhampa's personal relationship with His Holiness enabled him to obtain a private audience on request. Meeting the Dalai Lama had been a desire of Jon's for some time, ever since he had read his works, heard him speak, and been inspired by his teachings.

After Jon and Jhampa became acquainted, Jhampa generously invited Jon and a small group of Jon's friends to be included in the next scheduled audience with His Holiness at his residence in Dharamsala, India. The group that was finally chosen by Jhampa and Jon consisted of three students of Jhampa's who were practicing Buddhists and three academic-type friends of Jon's who were interested in Buddhism not as a religion but as a path of personal psychological growth and spirituality. All were inspired by the simplicity and the humanity of the Dalai Lama's teachings and would probably have said that they were seeking a better life for themselves and for others.

In retrospect, the Buddhists were perhaps better prepared for the changes that took place in the three weeks of the trip. The two of us were not prepared. Neither of us could have predicted how a short time in a remote location would change the course of our professional and personal lives.

The original idea was innocent enough: go to Dharamsala, meet with His Holiness the Dalai Lama, and ask permission to write a book using his teachings to help couples improve their relationships. Since we are licensed marriage and family therapists and had met while serving on the board of the International Association for Marriage and Family Counselors, we figured that combining our expertise could result in a relationship-improvement book that people would find helpful.

However, that book was never written. Once we returned from India, we tried to write the book we had originally intended to write, but the personal changes we had experienced made it impossible. No matter how hard we tried, the words would not come. We wrote drafts, rewrote drafts, changed the focus, talked by phone, e-mailed, met at conferences, and even traveled across the country for the explicit purpose of getting the book off dead center.

Nothing worked. We couldn't come up with an approach that was interesting enough to propel us through the long, arduous task of completing a book. It wasn't the work or the writing that kept us from going forward; between us, we have written almost sixty books (Jon has written fifty-five of them). The problem was that the interest and the energy just weren't there. Our passion and our focus had shifted; our hearts were elsewhere.

Finally, partly in despair, we deeply and honestly examined the experiences we had had in India and what they meant to each of us, and it was through this honesty that we discovered a poignant connection that we were able to identify as the source of our distraction. Raw candor revealed that we shared more than years of experience in academia and professional organizations, more than a desire to help others improve their marriages or love relationships, and more than a desire to publish another book. We shared a transformation that had come to completion in India that made anything but abject honesty impossible.

Words, whether written or spoken, wouldn't come unless they were honest words, vulnerable words, and intimate words about a topic we had never explored personally or professionally—words that began with the admission that our unspoken, shared experience was a profound loneliness that had been with both of us all of our adult lives. It was in India, unbeknown to each other, that we had begun to see a way out. The path became clear to both of us; in retrospect we see that it is a path on which we had already been walking individually, along parallel trails. Once the words "I am lonely" were spoken, the energy flowed and the pages of this book were written.

This book is divided into three parts. In Part I we tell the story of how we discovered the depth of our loneliness while on a trip to India to meet the Dalai Lama. We talk about loneliness and its prevalence, and we start the process of never being lonely again by introducing the teachings of His Holiness that reveal the path away from loneliness. In Part II we provide five questions that will help you to look at the core elements that create loneliness. In Part III, we discuss how to turn away and stay away from a life of loneliness by following the Middle Way.

Five years after our trip to India, our lives look and feel very different. The details of that difference are described in the chapters ahead. The bottom line is a promise we can make to you: if you know what it's like to be lonely—whether for a moment, a month, or a lifetime—there is a clear way out. As we share our personal experiences with loneliness as well as the story of our time in India, we will also share the path, the steps, and the lessons we learned through our travels to guarantee that you will never be lonely again.

Part One

The Depth of Loneliness

Three weeks in India gave us a generous amount of time to simply focus on being present in a mindful fashion. In addition, we spent most of each day surrounded by people who were doing the same thing. The waiter who served us breakfast, the man who swept the streets, and, of course, the Tibetan monks who were everywhere all seemed to be mindfully doing one thing at a time. This sounds so simple, but it was powerful. Crazy wisdom tells us that the simple act of doing less gave us more.

What doing less gave us was time to be mindful about the Four Noble Truths, the basic principles of Buddhism, and to begin to apply them to our lives. (1) If life is suffering, what is *my* suffering? (2) If suffering comes from attachment, to what am I attached? (3) If there is an end to suffering, how can I make it end? And if there truly is a way out of suffering, (4) show me the way!

While meditating on the First Noble Truth, life suffering, we began to identify our own brand of suffering as a longing that seemed to stalk us all the way to India. Sitting with our thoughts and feelings, watching them move in and out with our breathing, coalesced into a defining moment when the suffering took on the name of loneliness. That took some time to soak in.

Once we identified loneliness as our own form of suffering, the Second Noble Truth was waiting around the corner. We began to focus on the fact that suffering comes from attachment, or desire. When you read those words, they don't seem to have much impact, until you meditate on the fact that loneliness comes from your own desires, attachments, and clinging. When you experience your thoughts and feelings changing at will, pow! The paradigm shifts, the lightbulb goes on in your head, and you get it: *I'm creating this.* That moment changes you forever. Once you've changed, the way out becomes clear: *If I am causing it, I can fix it.*

After this realization, the Third and Fourth Noble Truths become more clear: there's an end to loneliness and there's a clear way out.

1

Lonely Times

PRAY THAT YOUR LONELINESS MAY SPUR YOU INTO FINDING
SOMETHING TO LIVE FOR, GREAT ENOUGH TO DIE FOR.

—Dag Hammarskjöld, former U.N. secretary-general

Pat's Story

During the loneliest times in my life, the mantra in my head went something like this: "Nobody knows me, and nobody wants to know me." I went through my days longing for someone to reach out and grab me, engage me, and draw me fully into life. I wanted to be touched, known, and experienced, but I didn't know how to make that happen. I felt alone, isolated, and empty, but that didn't make sense. How could I feel empty when I was so busy and productive? How could I feel isolated when I was married to a fine man, had two healthy and bright children, and was surrounded by friends and acquaintances? My loneliness didn't make sense, but it was real, because despite my best efforts, my connection to others, even those I loved, seem to hang by a thread.

Remembering the lonely times fills me with deep regret now, because I believe that I missed many important times in my life by not being present. I was there physically but not emotionally or intimately. I was disconnected from me and everyone else. Reflecting back, I can still

3

conjure the sensation of watching my life pass by on television, once-removed from reality. It's a surreal experience to be in a room where everyone seems to be relating, having a real life, connecting and reconnecting, and I am not.

I wonder now if anyone ever noticed my loneliness. Yet if someone had asked me, "Pat, are you lonely?" I probably would have said, "No." The loneliness was just too painful and embarrassing to acknowledge. Being lonely made me feel like a failure, as though something were wrong with me. I had spent much of my early life fearing that people would feel sorry for me, and I didn't want to be pitied or somehow seen as damaged goods.

Furthermore, I wasn't very aware; contemplation and self-examination were not part of my life. I didn't want to look at myself too closely; in fact, I kept moving from sunup to sundown just so I wouldn't be aware. I didn't want to be aware of the fact that I couldn't let anyone in or that I didn't know how to really connect with anyone—even my own husband and children. The movie inside my head did not include a picture of me as lonely, yet the loneliness was visceral. I walked around with a feeling of longing, as though I were missing something vital.

We once had a cat whose only kitten died shortly after birth, and afterward she walked around the house crying, going from room to room looking and searching. It was heartbreaking to watch her. That is what my life felt like so many, many times during the loneliness, especially in the morning and the evening, when it was the worst. I couldn't stay in bed once I awakened because the loneliness would take over, so as soon as I felt it coming I'd jump out of bed and get busy. At night I'd have to read or watch TV to distract my mind from going to the place of longing that is so real it can almost make you sick to your stomach.

As trying as all this was, however, it took years before I even questioned my state. I just thought that this is my life and I have to deal with it. But I didn't know how to make it better. If only I had been given a book like this; to realize that there was a clear way out would have made such a difference and would undoubtedly have prevented a lot of heartache and regret, because my loneliness and my lack of skills to manage it left a path of destruction through the first half of my life.

When I did start taking a closer look at myself, it was a little bit like a takeoff on an old country-western song: I was looking for answers in all the wrong places. Like many women and some men, I looked first at my primary relationship to find the cause of my suffering. This was long before author Dan Kiley coined the phrase *living together loneliness* (LTL), but I fit his profile perfectly: I was unhappy; I was unable to turn to my husband when I felt bad, because in my mind I wasn't supposed to have needs; I felt isolated and alone; and the only time I felt anywhere close to normal was when I was extremely busy—but even busyness was losing its solace. The loneliness was becoming more profound, and I had nowhere to turn. I finally left my marriage because I thought that it was the source of my misery. Yet even though I left the relationship, I took my loneliness with me. This was the beginning of many regrets.

Now I was a single parent, alone, and even more lonely. I could write a book about the dangers of dating and mating when you are lonely. Suffice it to say that it is not a good emotional place from which to make life decisions. Once again, I was looking in the wrong place to find the answer to my longing. To avoid the terror of being alone— because I now thought that being single was the cause of my lonely feelings—I ignored my values and my good common sense, just to have a man in my life. Score another regret.

When the next relationship didn't quell my loneliness, I started looking deeper. I went into therapy, reviewed my childhood, and confronted my history of neglect as well as my family history of divorce and alcoholism. Blaming my parents only made me bluer. By this time both of my parents had been dead for more than a decade, so at least I didn't blame them in person. I now have a much more compassionate understanding of their lives.

The next wrong place I looked for the source of my loneliness was a belief that I was depressed. Don't get me wrong, I believe that depression is a reality; some people are even born with a genetic predisposition for depression, a neurotransmitter deficiency that is very real. Others form thought patterns early in life that lead to a depressive state. Still others experience trauma, which physically changes your brain and requires treatment with medication and therapy. But there is a marked difference between depression and loneliness. Depression is a state; loneliness is a drive. I was diagnosed with depression and took the medication, but the misery remained. Medication doesn't alleviate loneliness. I was treating the symptoms rather than the source of my suffering. I muddled along this path for years. Another regret.

Finally, after years of struggle, I started to get the message: I had to do something different, try another path. About the same time I came across *The Art of Happiness* by the Dalai Lama. Maybe the student was ready, so the teacher came. I began reading the Dalai Lama's ideas, which were complementary to both the biblical teachings I had learned from Christianity and my clinical training in counseling. I was immediately drawn to the practicality of the Dalai Lama's approach. When he wrote that "monks can practice for years without ever clearing their minds completely; just sitting in a quiet place is a form of meditation," I thought, *I can do that!* When I read "Where Buddhism and science conflict, Buddhism must give way," I was blown away. I was further impressed when he said, "If you are from the West [and a Christian heritage], practice Christianity!"

The Dalai Lama's magnanimous approach and simple suggestions encouraged me to try a few of his ideas. I started with some basic forms of meditation; I began slowing down, paying closer attention, and being more aware. I learned to be more comfortable with doing less. I found a community of friends who embraced a more contemplative way of life. Then, when Jon invited me to go to India and meet with His Holiness, it felt right—like the next right thing to do. My life had been changing little by little, but little changes have big results, and everything came together in India. I'll tell you more about my journey as we go along, but first let's read Jon's reflections on his experience with loneliness.

Jon's Story

I have a privileged life; not much seems missing: professional success, a marriage of more than forty years, five successful children, good health, a history of world travel and adventure, and many lifelong friends. What do I know about loneliness? I pursued and found the American Dream. I was even an accomplished long-distance runner. I thought that I was facing loneliness each day and winning. So what was wrong? The answer lies in a fundamental question: Who am I? Really, who am I? Can I be that successful and yet feel unfulfilled and empty? What values are really important? What have my intentions been? Can I do the right things for the wrong reasons or the wrong things for the right reasons? Can I be attached and yet alone? When am I happiest? I had been doing everything right and yet felt wronged.

The American Dream is shallow, hollow, and empty. Happiness and success are directly related to the Dow Jones average, but the more I accomplished materially, the more detached I felt. To reduce this feeling I worked harder at doing what I know. Maybe I should write another book? Run an extra mile? Strive for another award? Lose some weight? None of these are bad objectives, but they did not improve my situation or relieve my lonely feelings. Material and objective success seemed hollow.

Shakbar Tsodruk Rangdrol, a great Tibetan yogi (1781–1851), once said, "To taste the full spread of the joys of samsara [the cycle of life, death, and rebirth caused by karma], such as wealth and other pleasures, is like tasting poisoned food, licking honey from a razor's edge; in short, it is a jewel on the head of a rattlesnake; one touch and you're annihilated." Dan Gilbert, author of *Stumbling on Happiness*, states,

"Happiness is reached through detachment and giving and not getting." How is that part of the American Dream? French Buddhist monk Matthieu Ricard states, "Nothing goes right on the outside when nothing is going right on the inside."

I went to India with a simple plan: to get permission from one of the world's most beloved people, His Holiness the Dalai Lama, to write a book based on his teachings with my colleague and friend, Pat Love. In addition, I was hoping to spend some quality time with my running buddy and longtime colleague, Addison, who was traveling with me. In India, however, things were not as I anticipated. As I stated, the world has treated me well, so I just assumed that everything would go as planned on this trip. It didn't take long for me to realize that the trip was going as planned—but I wasn't.

At first I thought that my lack of adjustment was due to the frenetic nature of Delhi, the city I flew in to, contrasted with the serene atmosphere of Dharamsala, where we were to have our meeting with the Dalai Lama. After all, we went from one of the largest cities in the world, teeming with people, animals, and vehicles, to one of the most tranquil places on Earth. I soon realized, however, that it wasn't the contrast between Delhi and Dharamsala; it was the contrast between doing and dropping out. For three weeks in India I dropped out of my element; things didn't work in predictable Western fashion. I was out of my comfort zone. I remembered a Finnish proverb, "Happiness is a place between too little and too much." I had been living with way too much, and these people seemed to live with way too little. I found myself somewhere in between—but I wasn't happy.

My second thought was that the altitude might be causing my change in attitude. Life at 6,000 feet felt different. But I had been in the mountains many times before, and I was quite sure that what I was experiencing wasn't caused by the fact that there was less oxygen getting to my brain. In a sense, my brain felt fuller than ever: full of the majesty of the Himalayan foothills; full of the music and the chanting from various sources around town; full of the comfort and the sense of community as I encountered people walking to the temple for their daily prayers. My body and my soul were being nourished by the daily cool breezes, the delicious vegetarian food, and the overwhelming calm of this way of life.

Nevertheless, there was an internal discomfort staying with me. Perhaps it was just the anticipation of meeting the Dalai Lama. No—it felt more like a change coming from within, not anxiety from without, and even after the audience with His Holiness, I still felt the internal shift taking place. The three weeks in India was serving as a period of reflection about my entire life. I had dropped out, but how would I drop back in?

Subtle Changes Back Home

As soon as we returned home, people wanted to know, "Well, how was it? What was it like being with the Dalai Lama?" Words can't adequately describe the experience. Yet even though words fail, actions don't. People close to us began to see the changes, perhaps before we did. We were calmer, more content, and more in contact with ourselves and others. People who might have felt excluded by missing out on the trip to India felt comforted by how present we were in our relationships with them. We didn't come home bragging about the unique experience we'd had. Instead of pride, there was presence. Basically, we just came home and went on with our lives, but in a more connected fashion. We weren't even fully aware of the changes that had taken place in India until we were faced with the reality of writing this book.

As we mentioned earlier, it took several years to understand why we couldn't come back home and immediately begin writing the book we had intended to write: we weren't the same. Neither of us had the heart for the former project, and the unrest that had previously driven our busyness wasn't there. When you don't have anxiety fueling your engine, you need another source of motivation. Before going to India, we would have jumped right in, written a book, and moved on to the next project. But now we couldn't do it. We were no longer just doing; we were living. We were calm and more content.

It wasn't that we were sitting around meditating all day or leading awareness retreats; we were simply going about life in a different fashion. We were still productive but not pushing. After months and months of avoiding the subject, we admitted that we were no longer the same people who had agreed to write the original book and therefore could not go through with it. This was a tough admission, because we like to pride ourselves on following through with our professional commitments, and ours was first and foremost a professional relationship. We had committed to writing the book, and His Holiness had given us permission, so what was stopping us? We finally realized that even though we couldn't write the book we had intended, this didn't mean that we couldn't write a different book—a book based on the changes we had experienced in India. We agreed to shift the focus, but neither of us initially brought up the subject of loneliness.

For Jon, his experience upon returning from India was similar to how he imagined Rip Van Winkle must have felt after waking up from a twenty-year sleep. "I was so caught up in living the American Dream," he explains, "that I never questioned my daily decisions. My wife, Laura, understood; she frequently urged that I spend more time with the kids or take some time off work, but I kept right on working long hours and completing project after project without any thought about what I was missing or what was fueling my mania. India provided the wake-up call, and I discovered my senses, as Jon Kabat-Zinn stated in his book *Coming to Our Senses*. I realized, at least at some level, that I had created a life that was anchored in loneliness. I began to ponder how I could continue to be a caring provider without all the busywork required. How could I make the shift from living a life based on corporate values to one based upon my personal values?"

Once our focus had shifted from a book about other people to a book about us, we became more energized, but the stakes became higher. How much do you reveal about your personal experience? Where do you draw the line between a professional book and a personal book? How much do you tell, what will the other person think, and is there a common thread between us that would hold a book together? By this time, we had been avoiding the book for almost three years, and we knew it was now or never. The time to make a decision was here.

Imagine the following scene. We had just finished conducting a weekend workshop at the Esalen Institute in Big Sur, California. (If there is a more beautiful place on Earth, neither of us has seen it.) We were tired from the weekend; our friends and our families were waiting for us to finish so they could depart. We had reserved two hours to spend making some decisions about the book, and the clock was ticking. One hour and fifteen minutes into our precious time, we were still sitting on a bench looking out at the ocean. No decisions had been made; there was silence, and then Pat began to tell a story.

You know how you sometimes tell a story or an anecdote and you don't even know why you are telling it? As we were pondering where to go with the book, given our individual changes, Pat began relating, for no apparent reason, an incident she had read about Oprah Winfrey's first meeting with Nelson Mandela, the antiapartheid leader and former president of South Africa. It was a peak experience for Oprah, one of the most famous people in the world, to finally get to meet her hero, someone she had held in the highest esteem all of her adult life. At a quiet moment during their meeting Oprah asked Dr. Mandela, "What can I do to help?" He thought a moment and then replied, "I want *you* to build a school for girls." Oprah quickly responded, "No problem." She reached for her checkbook and continued, "How much do you need?" Mandela looked her in the eyes and said, "No. I want *you* to build a school for girls." The emphasis on the word *you* made all the difference. He wanted her presence, her energy, and her involvement. Oprah did as he asked, and the rest is history.

The Oprah Winfrey Leadership Academy for Girls opened south of Johannesburg, South Africa, in January 2007.

After Pat shared the story, we were quiet for a few moments. We sat looking at the ocean, each wondering, "Is there a lesson in that story for us? Should we put more of our presence, our energy, and our involvement into the book?"

If we were making a movie of our "Aha!" moment—when we realized that we were talking about writing an honest book about the real lessons we learned in India—first there would be dramatic music and a camera close-up. You'd see beads of sweat, dilated pupils, and the abject fear of vulnerability. Then you'd hear us—two people who get paid to talk for a living—mumbling and searching through a dictionary before ultimately spitting out the truth about our history of loneliness and the way out of loneliness, which had become clear on the trip to India.

We wondered aloud, "Would we be willing to share with others what we have barely been willing to share with each other?" With trepidation, we agreed that yes, we would be willing to share. Once the decision was made, the dialogue began. "What really happened in India? Why are our lives different? What is the key ingredient that generated such a difference?" Before our two-hour time limit was up, we had our initial answer.

The significance of India was that we had left loneliness behind there. In India we not only saw the way out, we also lived the steps and integrated the process that guarantees that we will never be lonely again.

Blowing Our Cover

It's rather amazing that in all the years we had been colleagues and worked on joint projects, neither of us realized that we shared an inner experience of loneliness. In fact, once we became more honest, we admitted that each of us had admired the other, who seemingly had it all together and never felt lonely. Both of us were good at covering up.

"Like Pat and many other lonely people," says Jon, "I had developed a sophisticated cover to hide the fact that I was suffering from loneliness. My loneliness was buried so deep that no one seemed to suspect what was going on inside. As a man, I did not want to appear vulnerable, so I easily masked my feelings, laughed at sorrow, and used my intelligence to create power differentials with other people. I appeared thoughtful and kind, but not always for the right reasons. At some level I knew that I was covering up but that I was either in denial or afraid of opening Pandora's box and discovering the hidden contents. As Walt Whitman stated, 'There is that in me . . . I do not know what it is . . . but I know it is in me.' I knew that the vulnerable feelings of loneliness were there, but I didn't want to acknowledge them.

"I was well practiced in the cover-up," he continues. "I'd been practicing since boyhood. I knew that I used compensation, for example, to cover up my vulnerabilities. I compensated for being chronically sick by driving myself in athletics. As the youngest in my family I compensated for my age with intellectual pursuits and academic excellence. I pushed myself to achieve in all areas as a way to cover up the vulnerability I felt. I was always popular, I dated the prettiest girls, and I appeared to be anything but lonely. Laura and I have been married for more than forty years and have good relationships with each other, our children, and our families. Could it be that this was also compensation, a cover-up? Was I trying to be something that I wasn't—achieving, or maybe overachieving, in everything I did? Laura has said for years that I overdo everything.

"India provided the context, the special conditions, and the time for me to wake up and to go deeper into self-study," Jon concludes. "I wondered if this was the reason that so many of my age-mates came here in the 1970s to learn from gurus and swamis. I still remain puzzled and wonder the following: Why was loneliness such a revelation? How could I have such a huge blind spot? I'm a smart guy. I ought to know myself; I have meditated daily for three decades. What's up? The problem with using compensation as a cover-up for years and years is that it makes it very hard to understand who is the real me and to make the necessary changes to live my dreams and values."

Loneliness Is a Fact of Life

Loneliness is different for each individual, and the cover-up may be different, too, but loneliness is loneliness. Many of us feel trapped by our present plight and believe that if we can remove the loneliness, life will be happy and satisfying. For some people, the response to loneliness is to work harder to change the situation, yet this only leads to more frustration. As long as we are on the wrong path, hard work will not provide an answer.

We hope that it doesn't take you as long as it took us to understand that the first step away from loneliness is to accept that it is a fact of life. Pat wandered for years, trying this and that approach to a depression that was really loneliness. Jon spent decades achieving goals, making money, and accumulating status—all to avoid loneliness.

In his teachings, the Dalai Lama begins with the Four Noble Truths: (1) life means suffering, (2) the origin of suffering is attachment, (3) the cessation of suffering is attainable, and (4) there is a path to the cessation of suffering. These same truths apply to loneliness, and they served as guidelines to help us never be lonely again. We have adapted them as follows:

1. Loneliness is a fact of life. Nothing is permanent; there is loss and frustration.
2. The cause of loneliness is an attachment to transient things and a false vision of reality. In the real world, you can't hold on to what can't be held.
3. The cessation of loneliness is attainable.
4. There is a path to the cessation of loneliness. Loneliness ends when attachment stops and the world is accepted as changing or

impermanent. The path to the cessation of loneliness is laid out in the Eight Fold path: Right Livelihood, Right Intention, Right Effort, Right Action, Right Speech, Right View, Right Concentration, and Right Mindfulness.

There is loneliness with your name on it—it is a fact of life. You are ultimately alone, separated from others by the boundary of your skin. Your internal reality as well as your body belongs to you and you alone. No one can truly know how you feel or think or experience life. But being alone doesn't have to make you lonely; it's possible to feel quite connected and content all by yourself—at least for some time.

As a species, we humans greatly benefit from our ability to effectively spend time alone as well as with others. It would be highly inconvenient if we had to be with another person 24/7 in order to be stable, productive, and happy. Besides, many important activities require time alone: concentration, contemplation, reflection, focus, and integration. Nevertheless, the human brain requires a source of stabilization outside itself; in other words, we need other people in and out of our daily lives to feel safe and happy. This is because cooperation and support are two of our primary coping strategies. We are not the fastest species or even the strongest, but we have big brains, and we help one another. Because helping one another is connected to survival, our lives feel threatened when we are alienated from one another.

You would not die if you were left alone with food, water, and shelter —at least, not right away. Nevertheless, solitary confinement is used as a severe punishment for a reason: it's painful, and some research even claims to show that chronic feelings of loneliness will shorten your life. Loneliness is a response as well as a symptom, and it is designed to get your attention so you won't stay isolated beyond the point of benefit. Sometimes loneliness is a healthy signal, urging you to connect to others. At other times it's not. Sometimes it's a lot more complicated than that.

For that reason, we are not going to tell you to take up a hobby and get out more. If it were that simple, you would have done it already. In fact, those who battle loneliness will tell you that getting out can make you feel worse, not better. Instead, we are going to use what we call *crazy wisdom*.[1] Crazy wisdom is unconventional and therefore may *seem* crazy or strange, but trust us: it is wisdom rooted in centuries of practice. Using crazy wisdom, we are going to tell you to first defy common sense and pay attention to your loneliness, for your loneliness will serve as a guide to getting you to a state in which you will never be lonely again.

How Serious Is Loneliness?

When we finally admitted that loneliness had been part of our lives, it struck a strong emotional chord, but we weren't sure how many people would relate to the subject. It didn't take much research to find out that regardless of how many people actually admit to feeling lonely, there are millions who experience it. A report from the Harvard Medical School General Social Survey describes loneliness as "a very real and little-discussed social epidemic with frightening consequences."

To understand how prevalent this issue is, consider the following: In the United States, which ranks in the top quarter of nations with the highest frequency of loneliness, 25 percent of the people surveyed reported that they hadn't talked to anyone about anything important to them in six months. Another 19.6 percent said they have just one confidant. This means that close to 50 percent of Americans have no or only one close friend. This percentage has doubled since 1985.

Sixty percent of senior citizens say that they are lonely. Some of them have outlived their spouses and/or their friends. Others have children who have moved away (and taken the grandchildren with them). A growing number of adults have no children—by choice or otherwise.

---

1 Wes Nisker, *The Essential Crazy Wisdom*, Ten Speed Press, 1990.

Aging can bring physical disabilities, which make connecting with people outside one's neighborhood more difficult. In the United States today, someone turns fifty every seven seconds, 70,000 people retire every day, and by the time this book is published, 50 percent of the population will be over age fifty.

This "fifty over fifty" is a first in our nation. The population is changing. Neighborhoods are changing. Even if you stay in the same location, all your neighbors won't. Eleven percent of the population moves in any given year. So if you stay put for ten years, your whole neighborhood can change drastically. All of these changes can contribute to loneliness, but it's not just older folks who experience loneliness. Young people are reporting loneliness in growing numbers.

Because the average age of marriage is now later, more young people are living alone longer. In the United States during the 1950s, about 10 percent of households had only one person in them, and these were primarily widows. Today, 25 percent of households contain one person. Some people live alone because they prefer it, but others are living alone because they don't feel close enough to anyone else to want to share living space. A whopping 33 percent of people in their twenties move to a new residence every year, and they change jobs seven times during that age decade. No wonder 40 percent move back home with their parents at least once. It's not just finances that motivates them—it's support and contact.

Loneliness isn't limited to those who live alone, however, and many people who live by themselves are very happy and not at all lonely. We should be careful not to confuse *alone* and *lonely*; they are not synonymous. In contrast, many people who live with a partner, a family member, or a roommate feel desperately lonely. Just because you have people around you doesn't mean that you don't experience loneliness. In fact, the loneliest night you may ever spend could be lying next to someone you love. A surprising number of married people, as well as couples who live together, report that they are lonely. Just because two people live under the same roof doesn't mean that they feel connected or are free from the pangs of loneliness. As you will see in the rest of this book, loneliness comes in many forms, and having a partner doesn't guarantee that you won't experience it.

Whether you live alone or with someone, whether you are married or single, the situation today is that the number of people who provide social support and friendship seem to be shrinking in numbers. *Time* magazine recently reported that the number of people whom we count among our closest friends shrank, on average, from three friends to two in the past decade. Even if you have one or two people on whom you can rely and in whom you confide, overreliance on them can put undue pressure on the relationships and cause distancing—which can lead to loneliness.

In addition, despite the fact that many people have hundreds of virtual "friends" on Facebook, the number of real friends has dropped in numbers. Even in this time of advanced mass communication and social media, we remain accessible but not engaged. You can't snuggle up to an iPhone with much comfort or consolation. In fact, the more we limit our connections to technology, the lonelier we become.

Although staying in touch through technology certainly has its advantages, it can easily give you a false sense of intimacy—and it has an addictive quality. For example, because there is gratification in chuckling at a picture of a friend caught in an awkward situation, there's a constant temptation to log on to Facebook. It's not uncommon for the more compulsive cyberspace fans to have a dozen or more online services and to subscribe to scores of information feeds. They blog, tag, text, and tweet up to twenty hours a day.

In terms of addictive tendencies, no conversation about cyber relating would be complete without mentioning massively multiplayer online role-playing games (MMORPGs). One of the most popular MMORPGs, World of Warcraft (WoW), reportedly has more than 10 million subscribers per month. Wow for WoW. Online chatting is

full of stories of people flunking out of school, failing in their relationships, and even ruining their careers because of WoW. It's not unusual
for players to spend eight hours a day playing; that's one-third of your
life. Players and former players acknowledge that the game was designed
to be addictive, and it has succeeded immeasurably.

Second Life (SL), an online virtual world, has even more users
than WoW, according to some reports. The number of users may be
unknown, but SL has a fascinating promo: "Second Life, a place to
connect, shop, work, love, explore, and be different; free yourself, free
your mind, change your look, and change your life." That's a tall order.
One of our acquaintances spends most of his waking time chatting or
instant-messaging (IMing) on Second Life, which makes Second Life
his first life.

Relating in cyberspace can be fun, but the problem is that it leaves
you wanting more. The pleasure you get from gaming, chatting, IMing,
tweeting, or texting is short-lived, so to get much real enjoyment you
have to do it over and over and over again. One cyber exchange leads
to another, and pretty soon you look up and see that you've missed not
only your dentist appointment but a chunk of your life as well.
Ironically, the people who benefit most from social media are those
who already have friends. Technological relating tends to make the
lonely lonelier. One study showed that the boost you get from being
friended on Facebook is minimal, whereas being defriended is painful.
So, as in sports, losing feels worse than winning feels good.

When you are in touch all day long through technology, it gives the
illusion that you've been in relationships. The problem is you haven't,
really. Regardless of whether you are friend-rich or friend-poor, the
biggest problem with relying on the social media for connection is that
it is no substitute for face-to-face relationships. Plus, people online
sometimes make up false identities, so the relationships that you think
you have in cyberspace might not even be real. On the contrary, even a
short in vivo visit with a friend can leave you satisfied and ready to be

productive until your next get-together. It's additive but not addictive.

We are social creatures; this is a biological fact, and it is this need to socialize that provides the fuel that propels us into cyberspace through our desktop computers, laptops, mobile phones, and iPads. As electronic media have become more sophisticated and we have become more adept at using the many iterations of it, we have learned to communicate quite complexly with one another, even at a distance. Frequent texters can pick up subtle cues, interpret nuance, detect emotions, and decipher intentions, all from 140 characters or fewer.

Nevertheless, the most sophisticated electronic message, even one replete with video, sound, and three dimensions, cannot replace face-to-face, skin-on-skin sensations. Watching a kiss onscreen will never replace kissing in person; the same with intimacy. Having someone empathize with you in a text message isn't the same as having someone empathize with you face-to-face. The limbic resonance—the experience of seeing, feeling, hearing, smelling, and even tasting the experience of someone understanding you—is different from reading about someone understanding you. Five senses are better than one. They make a more memorable impact and reinforce the fact that you are not alone.

Years ago T. S. Eliot warned, "Television enables millions of people to listen to the same joke and laugh at the same time—yet remain lonesome." Social media do the same. There's no substitute for face-to-face, intimate social exchange. We have to be present to exchange and engage. Presence, in every sense of the word, is the key to never being lonely again.

Loneliness comes in many different forms and seems to exist on a continuum from slight to profound. You will see in this book that there are five major sources of loneliness, and some are more obvious than others. Although a significant amount of loneliness is related to relationships that are less than gratifying (e.g., "I don't have enough close friends"), other forms are more internal (e.g., "I don't know what I want to be when I grow up").

Each form of loneliness is exacerbated by the current zeitgeist; it is truly more difficult to keep loneliness at bay in the twenty-first century. You can't tune in to the daily news without being reminded that we are living in stressful times. A significant number of people withdraw from the outside world to protect themselves from its unfriendly nature. Ironically, this withdrawal creates a breeding ground not only for loneliness but also for indifference and aggression—even violent crime. The more isolated we are from one another, the less we care. As more people care less, the world takes on an increasingly unfriendly nature.

So how do you connect in a disconnected world, in a world that values busyness over leisure, commerce over community, competition over cooperation, and getting over giving? The answer lies in (1) knowing the sources of your own brand of loneliness, (2) understanding that loneliness comes from a craving for or an attachment to the wrong sources, (3) believing that the end of loneliness is possible, and (4) following the proven strategies that alleviate loneliness. Although the experience of loneliness is universal and shared by millions, the path that leads in and out of loneliness will be yours alone. This book serves as a guide to help you discover your own course.

Your Own Brand of Loneliness

Since you are reading this book, we assume that you have experienced some form of loneliness. Perhaps you have wondered, why me? Why am I the one who feels so alone? Others seem to have so much more love, friendship, money, connection, happiness, and success. You might be asking yourself, why can't I be happy with what I have? Why do I feel lonely when others who look at my life would be grateful for what I have? These questions have challenged all civilizations for centuries. No time in history has been spared. We are sure that these are only a few of the many questions that loneliness generates for you. We hope you have already realized that you are not alone and that there are millions of people around the world feeling just the way you do at any given moment.

We are making a second assumption about you because you are reading this book: you are somewhat of an expert on suffering and loneliness. If this is true, we also assume that you would like to be an expert on living wisely. The fact that you are curious enough to explore this often-ignored subject of loneliness indicates that you have a level of awareness that can work to your benefit. The first secret to never being lonely again is found in learning how to be fully present and conscious with your loneliness. We learned in India that loneliness, with all its pain and suffering, is enriched (and sometimes dissolved) by concentrating on it and accepting it. It is necessary to accept the truth that "life happens" and that even under the best circumstances, suffering and loneliness might be just around the corner, preparing to visit.

After the experience in India opened our eyes to a deeper and more meaningful way of living, so many of our former beliefs and teachings became clear. For instance, we gained a deeper understanding of loneliness and that it comes in different forms. Even though we had frequently read Buddhist teachings about the Four Noble Truths and how life contains both joy and suffering and that everyone experiences both, it took the experience of India to help us understand that we were creating our own brand of suffering in the form of loneliness. Most important, we learned that there is a way of life in which suffering and loneliness end. While we were in India, each of us experienced a shift in awareness and understanding. Before India, we knew the words; after India, we knew the way.

We hope that our words and stories will help to propel you out of loneliness. However, we realize that this book will not succeed by words alone. For this book to be the antidote for loneliness, you will have to immerse yourself in the various activities, questions, and exercises that are offered. Eastern civilization produces many magical and mysterious results if we are open to the nonlinear experiences that are part of that way of life. It is necessary to set aside our Western, self-focused way of thinking, then remove pride and step into a place of vulnerability, as the two of us have already done in this book.

It may be crazy wisdom, but the first step in moving away from loneliness is to accept loneliness. We offer the first exercise below in case you are unclear about certain aspects of your loneliness. In Pat's loneliest times, if she had been reading this book, she would have skipped over any exercise that was offered. Busyness was her cover, and she was too scared to let go of it. In fact, as long as Pat stayed busy, she felt normal; if she stopped to rest or relax, she'd first feel anxiety, then loneliness.

If you share any part of this cover-up, we want to reassure you of three important facts. First, the way out of loneliness is *through* loneliness: feeling it, sitting with it, and noticing it. Second, you have survived while living with loneliness for quite some time, so you will certainly survive while recalling it, especially since this is in the act of letting it go. Third, the exercises we offer are powerful and will change your life for the better. All you have to do is give them a try. You don't even have to believe that they will work; even faking it will produce results that will delight you in a short amount of time.

Before you know it, you'll have what we called JNDs: just noticeable differences. These are the changes in your thoughts, feelings, and behavior that you've been longing for. We wouldn't ask you to do these exercises if we were not absolutely convinced that they will work positively for you. None of the exercises takes a long time; we know that you are busy. Please give them a try. These exercises have been selected from tens of thousands that have been passed from generation to generation for thousands of years in Buddhism.

Exercise 1: **Back to the Present**

The first of the Four Noble Truths is that suffering (in this case, loneliness) is a fact of life. This isn't just a statement; it's a directive and part of the formula for freedom. Accepting that loneliness exists has been a lifelong exercise for the two of us. We offer you a shortcut by helping you to be more present. Learning to be more aware and more present is a very important step in moving away from loneliness. In this exercise, we invite you to think inwardly, to learn to observe your internal reactions to life as they change from moment to moment. As you read the words in this book, notice your reactions, your thoughts, your sensations, and your posture.

In the practice of meditation, an upright posture is extremely important. Having a straight back is not an artificial posture; it is natural to the human body. When you slouch, you can't breathe properly.

Once you are sitting in a good posture, pay attention to your breath; just start noticing your breathing. Start with the exhalation, and as it dissolves, notice how you naturally begin the inhalation. Then your breath goes out again. Watch your breath flow in and out naturally like the waves on a seashore.

As you breathe in, become aware of your posture and notice that you are ready for another exhalation. Dissolve that exhalation and become aware of your posture; breathe in, dissolve the inhalation, and again become aware of your posture.

As you follow this process, you will notice occasional thoughts. When you become aware of a thought, simply say to yourself that this is a thought, then come back to your breath. Whenever a thought takes you away, simply say, "Thought" and return to your breath and your posture.

Choosing Our Thoughts

As you complete this exercise, you will probably have realized that in any given moment you have many different thoughts. Thoughts are just thoughts and not facts. If you are on autopilot or are unaware of your thoughts, you will accept the habitual ones, even if they do not represent your values, your best interest, or your sense of identity. With practice, mindfulness can help you to get off autopilot and to become aware of the various thoughts that pass through your mind in any given minute. Once you are aware, you can choose the thoughts that fit your values. We spent many years not realizing that we were not choosing thoughts that represented our values.

It really doesn't matter what thoughts you have. Just label them "thoughts" and return to your breath and your posture. Thoughts are not good or bad, virtuous or sinful; they are nothing but thoughts. They are not facts. When we are unaware of our thoughts because we are on autopilot, we treat them as facts and live our lives as though they were true. This happened to the two of us for many years. The goal of the previous exercise is to get off autopilot and start the process of becoming aware of our mind and how it works.

Remember that your posture will assist you to stay aware and focused in meditation.

Were you able to do it? You can even do the exercise as you read. Now look away and see if you can just do it naturally, breathing in and out, noticing your posture, noticing any thoughts floating by, and then coming back to your breath. How do you think your life might change if you practiced this often? What changes would you like to see happen?

Exercise 2: Out Through Loneliness

What do we mean when we say that the way out of loneliness is through loneliness? It is through the suffering of being lonely that you can travel to a place of connection, happiness, contentment, or love. Thousands of years of research have shown the way. To begin, you must not ignore your experience; on the contrary, you must embrace it. You can write about your loneliness (we highly recommend this), you can talk about it, and you can get a clear sensation of it. We are going to invite you to bring it into existence as you prepare to let it go.

As we talked to people about their experiences with loneliness, some of the same words and phrases kept showing up. See how your experience compares.

Many people described the sensation of loneliness as emptiness. A woman stated, "I feel hollow inside, like there is no essence to me." A man described himself as "unimportant" and said that although he was six feet tall, he still felt small and insignificant, as though he didn't matter to other people or to himself much of the time.

Invisibility was another description we frequently heard from people who have lived with loneliness. "I feel like I can walk through a crowd and no one will see me," said a mother of three children. A man in his early twenties stated, "I don't trust other people and I don't trust myself to stay connected to others, so it's a two-edged sword."

Other feelings we heard described were despair, hopelessness, disconnection, seclusion, being unloved, meaninglessness, and even resentment. The man who expressed resentment said that he resented people who were surrounded by friends and families, people he would see in public enjoying one another's company. He admitted that when he was walking at night, he would look in people's windows and would feel envious when he saw people sitting in the same house, watching TV together.

Describe your experience of loneliness. Be graphic; go into detail. Use all the words and phrases that have ever applied to the times you've felt lonely in your life. Write down your experiences.

We ask you to complete this exercise at least ten times and note the different results that appear each time. Accept whatever comes up. If you draw a blank, just describe the blank; if your mind wanders, understand that this is normal and gently come back to the exercise. Some have likened this process to peeling layers off an onion or taking apart a set of Russian nesting dolls. The uncovering of each layer or doll provides new observations. Learn to love and find comfort in this process. Do not worry about getting to the bottom; just accept that there is an abyss and that there is information available at each new level.

Exercise 3: **Embodied Loneliness**

In this exercise we want you to become aware of where loneliness resides in your body and to determine the bodily sensations that accompany the feelings of loneliness. Your body often provides clues to the strength and depth of your feelings. When we asked people, "Where does loneliness reside in your body?" many answered that it resides near the heart or in the pit of the abdomen.

"Feels a lot like homesickness," one man offered, "like when I was a kid and went to camp for the summer." A very successful female executive told us, "When I get lonely, it's like my heart is breaking; it actually hurts. Loneliness is heartache." A retired coach said that he sometimes feels burdened by the weight of his own body when he's lonely. For Pat, loneliness can wash over her like a wave of fear, or it can wake her up in the middle of the night with a lightning strike in the solar plexus. During the day, the fear of loneliness can drive Pat to incessant busyness. As long as she is preoccupied, the fear might stay at bay, but relaxation can cause the anxiety to rise up and remind her that she is alone, disconnected, and helpless to do anything about it.

It is important to know your own pain of loneliness, to give it words and know where it resides. This exercise will help you to become aware of lonely times, for we tend to experience loneliness in the same ways.

Where does loneliness live in your body? Can you get a vision of it? Can you make the sensation stronger and give it more life? Pay close attention to your answers. If you are having difficulty, ask where exactly your loneliness is located. What color is it? What shape does it take? As you concentrate on your answers, repeat the questions and see if the loneliness changes or dissolves. Continue to focus on awareness of your inner world, both body and mind.

Exercise 4: **From Loneliness to Compassion**

Once you have identified the pain, the discomfort, or just the sensation of loneliness, as well as where it lives in your body, expand your mind to include others who are lonely. Use your common experience of loneliness as a bond, a bridge that connects two of you, at first, then extend it to include numerous others who are lonely.

Get in touch with your own experience of loneliness. Make the sensation stronger; feel it in your body. Now imagine that someone close to you has experienced loneliness. Let yourself be curious and concerned about his or her experience of loneliness and what it might be like. Let your mind reach out to this person. Recognize that the sensations are the same as yours, that loneliness lives in the other's body just as it lives in yours. Can you see it now in the facial expression? Can you recognize the body posture that carries loneliness? Acknowledge that you share this common experience. Feel the pain that the other person is feeling.

Now take on the pain and join it with yours. Imagine that you are bearing the burden for this person as well as for many others. Notice and feel others' burdens lift as you share their suffering. See the relief as they realize that they do not suffer alone. Feel your own sense of relief as you honor the experience of loneliness.

This exercise is worthy of daily practice. In fact, if you concentrate on this process repeatedly, you will feel a shift in your perception of other people as well as in your experience with loneliness. If you do only one exercise, this should be the one.

Can You Accept Compassion?

As you continue to ponder the importance of the previous exercise, make it even more powerful by asking these questions: Can you open your mind to the fact that others might be willing to take on your burden of loneliness just as you have taken on theirs? Can you accept the compassionate acts of others? Can you let others share this burden with you?

Loneliness is a drive that can move you toward connection, congruence, and authenticity. The journey away from loneliness begins with the awareness of loneliness and the courage to tell the truth. We encourage you to honor the experience of loneliness; it can be your compassionate friend, for it connects you to millions of people in the world.

Responding to Loneliness

No one would choose a friendless
existence on condition of having all the
other things in the world.

—Aristotle

If you are lonely, the question is how you will respond to it. Will you smother it with busyness? Will you let it paralyze you? Will you translate it into self-pity? Or will you use it to be compassionate toward others' suffering and share their burdens? What kind of a dance partner will you be with loneliness? In India we met many people who were separated from their families and other loved ones because they had migrated from Tibet to be close to His Holiness. Even though they were away from their support systems and clearly missed their loved ones, they seemed to dance with loneliness in a conscious and peaceful manner. Let us introduce you to one of our favorites.

Osal is a young Tibetan man in his early twenties who became our unofficial guide during our time in Dharamsala. He is a tall, thin guy with a big smile, sparkling brown eyes, and long black hair tied in a ponytail. Every day he would show up and serve as our social director and tour operator, easily taking care of the smallest details and making our day, no matter what the event, almost effortless. He knew how to make taxis appear magically; he knew the best and cheapest places to eat; and all the local merchants seemed willing to give him the very best deals on almost anything we might care to purchase. He had no sales pitch or agenda, except to do his best to make our time meaningful. He struck us as being quite authentic and caring.

As we got to know Osal, he began to share the details of his former life in Tibet and the treacherous journey he had taken over the Himalayas to seek freedom in India. He told us about sneaking out of his family home without saying good-bye to his beloved parents or siblings because he feared that if any of his family knew the details of his plans, they would be tortured for helping him to escape. In addition, he revealed, it wasn't safe to confide in anyone about his plans to leave, because even family members might be paid by the government to report those who were planning to defect.

As he described the ordeal of crossing the Himalayas with his small party of refugees, we were struck with the life-threatening challenge of making the journey. Because of the fear of being apprehended, the group hid during the day and traveled only at night, which made the trek far more dangerous because of the cold and the limited visibility. The refugees had very little food for the trip; since money and supplies were limited in Tibet, stockpiling food would have attracted attention. The journey out of Tibet was physically challenging and most taxing, but by far the most stressful part of the journey was living with the constant fear of being caught. The mental strain was even greater than the physical strain. Finally, Osal and his companions made it to Nepal, where they were detained and eventually released.

From Nepal, Osal made his way to India and the Tibetan resettlement center in Dharamsala. By the time he arrived in Dharamsala, his travel companions had gone elsewhere and he was completely alone. He couldn't write or phone home for support because he was afraid that contacting his family and friends in Tibet would endanger their lives. He was by himself in this new community, with no friends or acquaintances, but he wisely figured that if he was going to make contacts in the new location, he'd have to learn the language. So he inquired about classes and immediately began studying the local language, even though it meant walking several miles each day to the free school. Osal knew that he would need to communicate if he was going to make connections—the only way to keep loneliness at bay.

According to Osal, loneliness is an unavoidable part of life. Everyone, even the Buddha and the Dalai Lama, has experienced pain and loneliness. He reminded us that the Dalai Lama (arguably one of the happiest people on the planet) was taken from his family at a young age and then later from his country; His Holiness has been very open about the loneliness and sadness he felt with each of these events. In addition, Osal reminded us that loneliness can originate not only from external events but also from how we process and respond to those events in our minds. The mind is filled with emotions that can arise in reaction to what is going on around us. Loneliness becomes a problem when the untrained mind reacts negatively to life changes. Our mind clings to, craves, or grasps at a different event or outcome. We attempt to change the reality of life to fit the reality that we want. This clinging creates suffering.

Osal further revealed that long before he fled Tibet, he had begun training his mind. When we heard his story we were at first struck by the arduous nature of the physical trek across the Himalayas and the challenges one would face to train the body to endure such a journey. On second thought, however, we realized that the mind would require even more training than the body. To make the journey from your homeland, knowing that you were leaving everyone you love behind and most likely would never see them again would require a far different level of mastery.

We now find it most interesting that we had several conversations with Osal about leaving his family and living in exile even before we knew we were going to write about loneliness. In retrospect it now makes sense why so many of our conversations led to this subject; in some ways, we had been living in exile ourselves, trying to cover up our loneliness. We are still impressed with Osal and his story, but we are even more impressed with how his Buddhist mind responded to the loneliness long before he left his homeland.

Osal grew up being trained in the Four Noble Truths: (1) life means suffering, (2) the origin of suffering is attachment, (3) the cessation of suffering is attainable, and (4) there is a path to the cessation of suffering. He was well aware that leaving Tibet would create suffering. To think that he could leave all the people he loved as well as the land he loved and not experience pain, longing, yearning, or loneliness was unrealistic. Being separated from loved ones creates sadness; missing friends and family causes pain.

This is a fact of life and of relationships. When you love someone and get close to someone, you sign up for the possibility of pain. Thus, life means suffering. In some ways, suffering means that you've been in the game of life. If you drop out, there's suffering; if you get involved in life, there's suffering. Suffering is part of life either way. Osal knew that he would miss his friends and his family; he knew that he would be lonely. He also knew that he had a choice of how to respond to the loneliness.

The Second Noble Truth is that the origin of suffering is attachment. Here we need to make sure that the true meaning doesn't get lost in translation. *Attachment* means being invested in your own form of reality—investing in, expecting, and clinging to a particular outcome. When you are attached, or dependent on life going a particular way, and it goes another, disappointment occurs. Judging the event negatively creates the disappointment. Negative judgment is a choice. For Osal to expect to leave home and never miss anyone would mean being attached to an impossible reality. Expecting to leave home and never be lonely is clinging to an outcome that does not exist. To be away from loved ones and be lonely is logical. To judge this loneliness negatively creates suffering. You, like Osal, get to choose what to do about loneliness.

You can easily look at Osal's choice of coming to India and see that he came of his own free will. In a sense, he made an appointment with pain. There are, however, situations in life in which you are not part of the orchestration. Suffering comes when you have had no hand in causing it. Loved ones fall ill or die, partners leave, jobs are outsourced, and technology advances.

If selling videotapes is your business and DVDs start taking over the market, you can damn the DVD business, cling to the videotape business, and go broke, or you can accept reality, let go of your attachment to that business and way of life, and move on. Clinging to a videotape business in the age of DVDs will work in some places, but not many. You can believe that the origin of your suffering is the DVD business, but in reality it is your attachment, your clinging to the videotape business, that creates the suffering. You can't even rest in the assurance of the DVD, because even as we write, it is being replaced by streaming and who knows what next. The origin of suffering is attachment to transient things and denial of the very nature of life, which is impermanence.

Osal could make the trip to India, leave his loved ones and homeland, and know that he would again be happy, because he believed the Third Noble Truth: the cessation of suffering is attainable. The key to the cessation of suffering is to let go of unrealistic expectations and not let your mind wallow in loneliness or other forms of suffering. Setting your expectations in line with reality is a good start. A particular situation is happening, and I get to choose how I respond to it.

Osal used his loneliness to motivate himself. Earlier we mentioned that loneliness is a drive; it is designed to move you toward something. Osal learned the local language, volunteered his time to meet people, worked as an assistant to an elderly woman in exchange for rent, and learned the local attractions so he could become a tour guide. He also knew that his suffering was shared by the many people he had left behind. In his meditations he used his suffering to connect to and feel compassion for those back home. Most of all, he took comfort in knowing that there is a way to end suffering.

The Fourth Noble Truth is that there is a path to the cessation of suffering. We will go into more detail about the process that ends suffering in subsequent chapters. In summary, the end to suffering (and the end to loneliness) comes with living life on the Middle Way—avoiding extremes. Osal found the Middle Way. In Tibet he could not be educated, speak of his homeland, study its history, or have religious freedom; he could have been imprisoned simply for having a picture of His Holiness the Dalai Lama in sight. To Osal, this was an extreme. He left his homeland and the people he loved, but he knew that he would love again. He also knew that he would carry his love for his family over the Himalayas and into India. Thus, he chose the Middle Way.

The Four Noble Truths provide a clear path away from loneliness, and the first step, as we have emphasized, is to acknowledge that loneliness exists. Just think how our own lives might have been different if we had simply acknowledged that loneliness existed instead of running away from it all those years. The loneliness was there; we felt it, but we didn't sit with it, honor it, and acknowledge it. We were not mindful of our actions; we simply reacted.

We want to help you to move to a state in which you will never be lonely again by first encouraging you to be mindful of your loneliness. It sounds like crazy wisdom, but we ask you to trust us and come along.

Mindfulness, Suffering, and Impermanence

Buddhism states that to be free of suffering or to attain liberation, you must first understand how suffering affects you. You do this by being mindful of your reactions. Being mindful means that you focus on one thing at a time and do it on purpose. Mindfulness also includes being conscious of the consequences of your actions. You are aware, tuned in, and paying attention.

Liberation comes from experiencing and being fully aware of how your life is affected by what Buddhism calls *dukkha*, the impermanent nature of life. Anything that is not permanent, that is subject to change, is dukkha. Happiness, success, and beauty all fade with time. This doesn't mean that they are bad; we may enjoy them in the moment, but we must not cling to them or expect them to last forever. Liberation comes from accepting change; being mindful of your reaction to change; and practically speaking getting your expectations in line with reality.

Your team wins the championship—that's dukkha, because another season begins next year. The handsome face of your lover is dukkha, because he will not stay that way over time. Human beings are born and will ultimately die, dukkha. The ever-changing nature of life is dukkha. You create suffering when you expect the impermanent to be permanent.

The suffering associated with dukkha can come from many sources, such as loneliness, unhappiness, pain, inadequacy, failure, or disappointment. Buddhists are quite practical; they recognize that dukkha is part of life. A Westerner might say that "dukkha happens." The lesson doesn't end there, however; it's what happens *after* dukkha happens—how suffering affects you—that determines the ultimate outcome.

Even though we have used the term *suffering* to explain dukkha, there isn't really a satisfactory English translation for it. The words *disquiet, anguish, misery, frustration, discomfort, stress,* and *dissatisfaction* all apply, but each time you try to define it, another meaning emerges and you realize that you have missed an important element.

Dukkha, which may also be translated as *impermanence*, applies to all human beings: both sexes, all races, all ages, all religions. None of us wants to grow old and die. Disappointment and death bring painful experiences to anyone touched by them, but that is the nature of life. It's just a fact. It's dukkha. The richest person experiences dukkha as much as the poorest does. Dukkha is experienced by royalty the same as by the enslaved. Being isolated from someone you love is painful no matter how smart you are or how limited you are intellectually. Buddha simply said that there is dukkha; he could have said, "I am suffering, you are suffering, we all are suffering."

Buddhism is devoted to the end of suffering. Loneliness is one of the many ways in which we suffer. When the Buddha called suffering dukkha, he was referring to the mental experiences of discomfort, failure, loneliness, and disappointment. Buddhists learn at an early age that feelings of suffering are part of life, present at any given moment. Buddhists are taught to gain insight and knowledge about their suffering through being consciously aware and realizing that they have a choice of how to react to suffering.

Some suffering and loneliness originates from external events. We lose parents, partners, friends, jobs, and homes. Buddhists accept this as part of the deal of life. There's no sense in trying to avoid it, for it is part of everyone's existence. This concept is similar to the message of the Serenity Prayer by Reinhold Niebuhr: "God grant me the serenity to accept the things I cannot change, the courage to change the things I can, and the wisdom to know the difference."

Things change no matter how much we try to hold on. Bad times are followed by good times, which are followed by bad times, and so on. It is a fact that life is constantly changing. No matter how much we appear to be successful in life by dealing with challenge after challenge, we are really distracting ourselves from accepting change. We may be distracting ourselves on the outside, but on the inside, the nervous system processes and feels what we are attempting to ignore.

The Buddha thought that suffering is a mental event. There will be some pain, dukkha, that is part of life, but we can learn to react to it as we choose. When we are attached to life being as we wish and not as it is, we are living with a false vision of reality, and this false vision is a source of suffering. Buddha understood the difference between the pain of life and our reaction to it. We often view suffering as a sign of failure, inadequacy, or ineffectiveness. If you had your "game on," you wouldn't be such a loser and this never would have happened. You need to work harder and be smarter, and you can avoid all pain.

Wrong! Dukkha is part of life. Suffering is a fact of life. You don't get to live without it. To expect life to be perfect is a sure setup for unhappiness. If perfection is your expectation and your life has disappointing events that make it less than perfect, it's not the disappointing events that are the problem, it's your unrealistic expectations.

The two of us learned how much we suffer from all of our wants, needs, cravings, and responsibilities. By working so hard at meeting needs, fulfilling wants, and being super responsible, we were actually denying the dukkha in our lives and could not respond in a healthy way that represented our core values. We realized that we had been denying just how much stress, inconsistency, dissatisfaction, and loneliness was in our lives. We hid our suffering from others (as well as from ourselves) to avoid negative judgment. By hiding or ignoring, we have been ignorant. Awareness and acceptance is the antidote to ignorance.

We needed to learn to focus on and not ignore or deny the demands of life. That's right. We needed to become aware or mindful of the suffering, stress, distress, regret, and pain that is in our minds and our bodies. Understanding suffering through awareness made it possible to become clear about what was really happening in our lives. By knowing our minds, we began to know ourselves, and we began to live in congruence and harmony as we responded in a wise rather than a reactive fashion. The way out of loneliness is through it.

Being Mindful of Loneliness

Loneliness, like other forms of suffering, is part of life. Loneliness itself is not the problem; it is how you respond to it that determines the outcome. You are alone, a distinct entity separated from others by your skin, and you have to take action to be connected.

If you are aware that loneliness exists in your life, we congratulate you. You are so much farther along the path to freedom than we were for so many years. Ownership is the first step to liberation. Once you realize that loneliness exists, you have options in the way to respond. Like Osal, we have choices about how our minds react to loneliness, but we must start by noticing—that is, acknowledging that loneliness is a fact of life. Noticing is part of mindfulness, the conscious, moment-by-moment awareness of how your mind reacts to all of your experiences. By noticing your loneliness and how you react to it, you can learn how to mindfully respond rather than react.

We encourage you to be mindful of loneliness. This means to purposefully feel, experience, and let your mind dwell on being lonely. If you want the promise of never being lonely again, you first have to get a handle on your loneliness. Mindfulness practice will help you to do this.

Loneliness is part of everyone's life; it can't be avoided. When loneliness is suffering and not positive solitude, that is due to our own response. Mindfulness will help you to find the moment when you can choose happiness over loneliness.

Being Present in the Moment

Before we went to India, each of us had had the privilege of spending several days working with Jon Kabat-Zinn, the founder and former executive director of the Center for Mindfulness in Medicine, Health Care, and Society at the University of Massachusetts Medical School. We met Jon and his wife, Myla, when we were working on a DVD series called *Parenting with the Experts*. For this series, well-known authors and experts came to Chicago for three days of filming before a live audience.

During the course of the filming, we got to spend a great deal of time with the presenters. We picked them up at the airport, took them to dinner, checked them into a hotel, escorted them to the studio, and worked with them on the script, the camera work, and the content.

Through this experience we got to see the various professionals react and respond to several different circumstances: late planes, miscommunications, travel fatigue, time changes, filming pressures, and so on.

You might not be surprised to learn that the professionals weren't always so professional. But this was not the case with Jon and Myla Kabat-Zinn. What stood out immediately about them is how very present and thoughtful they are. If anyone embodies their teaching, they do. Getting to know the Kabat-Zinns greatly increased our interest in and respect for their work. Jon's is the most common name you associate with the practice of mindfulness in the United States. He, like his work, is accessible.

Jon Kabat-Zinn defines mindfulness as simply paying attention in a particular way. More than awareness, mindfulness means being present in the moment and paying attention in a nonjudgmental way—on purpose. Jon suggests several ways of practicing mindful meditation: sitting, standing, and walking. Often beginning with the breath, his mindfulness exercises focus on being in the present moment, suspending judgment, and noticing.

In India we found ourselves surrounded by people who were living in the moment in a mindful fashion. Right away we knew we weren't in Kansas anymore. Especially in McLeod Ganj (a section of Dharamsala), where we stayed before we had the audience with His Holiness, people were attentive and focused. In comparison to most Westerners, the shopkeepers, visitors, and hotel personnel were tuned in to what they were doing. The most noticeable difference in the people we encountered walking the streets and saying their morning prayers was their single-mindedness. They seemed to be doing one thing at a time.

It was so different from the multitasking multitudes we encounter each day in Austin, Texas, and Lake Geneva, Wisconsin. These people were focused and present. We didn't see the mania that we've come to accept as the norm in the West. Not once did we see someone walking with a friend while talking on the phone while pushing a baby stroller on the way to shopping. Are we idealizing the East? Perhaps. We do know that the difference in the atmosphere and cultural practice was noticeable.

Pat's suitcase didn't make it to Delhi, so all she had to wear were the clothes on her back. To compensate, she bought a traditional Indian tunic and pair of pants—in bright red. The airlines had given her a survival pack that contained a few toiletries and a white T-shirt. So with a little washing by hand every night, she was able to have clean underwear every day, but she wore the same red tunic and pants all the time. At some point it became necessary to wash the tunic and pants, so she put on her travel clothes, washed the outfit, and hung it on the rail of the hotel balcony to dry.

When she went to retrieve them some hours later, they were gone. We don't know whether the monkeys carried them off or the wind blew them away, but they were gone. She climbed down the hillside and searched through the woods, but the clothes were nowhere to be found. She figured they were gone for good. However, the next time she passed the front desk, the clerk behind the counter stopped her by holding up his index finger (he didn't speak English); then he reached behind the counter and brought forth her neatly folded tunic and pants. How did he know they belonged to her when he found them? He was mindful.

The atmosphere around Dharamsala did indeed feel different. There was a reverence and a single-mindedness as people went about their everyday lives, but there were also formal occasions to practice mindfulness. At specified times people would gather for meditation and chanting. Jhampa, our faithful Buddhist guide, arranged for us to take part in these sessions at different times throughout the day.

After several days of practice reinforced by the presence of other people doing the same, we started to understand better how we could train our minds to experience increased awareness. The mindfulness we practiced during the meditation times began to carry over into the ordinary events of each day. We became more focused, more single-minded, more present, and less distracted. Calmness came with the mindful practice, and we began to notice sustained attention as well as the ability to experience both positive and negative events without overreacting. We were beginning to understand how suffering is related to our attachment to a particular outcome, because we experienced being able to choose the outcome. We began to simply notice instead of judging. It was quite liberating to realize that we could choose how to process events and finally let go of both positive and negative experiences and just notice our responses without judgment. "Hmm, my clothes are gone," Pat observed.

Mindfulness is a way to help us become aware of our attachments to a particular outcome. In addition, mindfulness makes it possible to change our reactions to the outcome, which reduces our suffering. The awareness that comes from focusing on one thing at a time, on purpose, can be divided into three levels. On the first level, you become aware after the fact that you acted in a mindless fashion. Darn, I did it again! The second level of awareness is knowing that something is happening right now that you don't like, but it happens anyway. The third level, and the goal of mindfulness training, is to be focused enough to choose your thoughts and behaviors at any given moment. This is what Jon Kabat-Zinn calls "on purpose."

Monkey Mind

Focusing our minds on one thing at a time is a major part of mindfulness training. In the busy world in which we live, it is so easy to go through each day without awareness, just letting our thoughts jump from stimulation to stimulation. This bouncing has been referred to as "monkey mind" and is the opposite of mindfulness. When you are letting your mind run free like a monkey, the shiniest object gets your attention. It doesn't matter that your friend is pouring out his or her heart to you; if your cell phone rings, you jump to answer it, or if you see a car you like, you exclaim, "Oh, look at the new Prius!" It's so unrewarding to interact with someone who is in a state of monkey mind. It's as if you are not important. It's almost worse than being ignored. It's lonely.

If you don't understand the following joke, you may not be familiar with the concept of monkey mind. Consider yourself lucky if you have to get someone to explain it to you; it's one of Pat's favorite jokes, because she can relate to it 100 percent.

Two women were driving down the road when the one in the passenger's seat noticed that the driver had run a stop sign. *Wow*, the passenger thought, *that's dangerous. She didn't even notice. I wonder how I can point that out to her without hurting her feelings.* Before she could come up with the words, however, the driver ran a second stop sign. The passenger turned to the driver and blurted out, "Are you aware that you've run two stop signs?" The driver gasped, her jaw dropped, and she exclaimed, "Oh, am I driving?"

That's an extreme case of monkey mind. It's dangerous and too true to be entirely funny.

Exercise 5: Measure Your Monkey Mind

Are you someone who:	Never 1	Seldom 2	Sometimes 3	Often 4	Too often 5
Has frequent accidents	___	___	___	___	___
Forgets details	___	___	___	___	___
Rushes through activities to get them done	___	___	___	___	___
Daydreams and appears lost	___	___	___	___	___
Smokes, drinks, or eats without awareness	___	___	___	___	___
Is easily distracted	___	___	___	___	___

Attempts to do many things at once	___	___	___	___	___
Thinks a lot about the past	___	___	___	___	___
Wonders a lot about the future	___	___	___	___	___
Spends much time each day on autopilot	___	___	___	___	___
Says one thing while thinking of another	___	___	___	___	___

Doing One Thing at a Time

When was the last time you had an uninterrupted conversation with someone? Have you noticed how few people speak in complete sentences? Do you speak in complete sentences? Do you finish your thoughts? Do you finish others' thoughts? Mindfulness teaches you to do one thing at a time, with purpose and focus.

If you are intent on mastering loneliness, if your goal is to never be lonely again, then you must gain control of your mind. As Jhampa's teacher, Lama Yeshe said, "To become your own psychologist, you don't have to learn some big philosophy. All you have to do is examine your own mind every day. You already examine material things—every morning you check out the food in your kitchen—but never investigate your mind. Checking your mind is much more important." Once you check your mind and are in control, you can take your mind anywhere you wish. You have a choice of how to respond to the world and what it brings your way. Mindfulness is an invaluable friend.

Mindfulness meditation is similar to an exercise we learned in India that we call the Tibetan Two-Step; it's a great way to cure monkey mind. It involves concentrating your attention on an object, a word, or a phrase in order to become aware of how your mind reacts to what it experiences. With practice, you will be able to use concentration and mindfulness together and remain focused rather than jumping among various thoughts and feelings. Being purposeful with your mind will enable you to transform loneliness at any given moment.

Exercise 6: The Tibetan Two-Step

The Tibetan Two-Step is a very simple mindfulness meditation, with two parts, that involves learning to be aware in the present.

Step one: Notice that you are breathing. Since you are reading this book, you must be breathing and already doing this step in the mindfulness exercise. Congratulations. We told you it was easy.

Step two: Focus your attention on the present moment, beginning with your breath. Pay attention to the air coming into your body and going out of your body. Sometimes it helps to breathe in through your nostrils and out through your mouth. Pay attention to how the air feels as it enters your nose and fills your lungs. Then exhale and tune in to the air leaving your body as your shoulders and muscles relax. As you continue to focus on your breath, with each and every exhale feel your body relax. As you notice the sounds around you, let them float into the distance and come back to the breath and relax. If thoughts or feelings enter your awareness, let them float into the distance and come back to the breath. With the exhale let your face muscles relax. With the next exhale let your shoulders relax. Exhaling again let your chest muscles relax. Letting go of the breath, let your stomach muscles relax. Feel your thighs and calves relax as you exhale again. Let relaxation flow over your body as you focus on the breath. Begin to become aware of the noises and sounds, the smells and fragrances, the texture of your clothing, the support of the chair or cushion, the temperature of the room, all the while breathing and taking in the present moment.

Keep repeating these two simple steps. The only way to do this wrong is to not do it. If your mind wanders, just bring it back to your breath. It's really this simple and powerful.

There are thousands of variations on the Tibetan Two-Step, and we will suggest a few as we continue the journey out of loneliness.

Exercise 7:

Focusing on Your Breath with a Mantra

There are many ways to focus on your breath: counting, noting the speed of your breathing, or using label pairs like *peace* and *love* or *in* and *out*. It can be helpful to pair a word or a mantra with each breath. Words like *om* and *peace* have been favorites for centuries. Repeating a word or sound focuses your mind and if you combine the sound with the experience of relaxation, it will train you to focus and relax just by uttering or even hearing the sound.

The mantra can become your personal point of attention or focus. Use words to help you visualize what can be: Breathe in *health* and out *sickness*; breathe in *energy* and out *fatigue*; breathe in *love* and out *anger*; breathe in *happiness* and out *sadness*; or breathe in *connection* and out *loneliness*.

Wakefulness and a Purposeful Life

The breathing exercises (1, 6, and 7) may be difficult at first. It might take several attempts for you to be able to breathe in and out without losing focus. When you realize that your mind has wandered, gently bring it back to the breath. Some days will be better than others. Learn to accept whatever happens, knowing that you are learning about yourself and how your mind works. It is natural for the untrained mind to wander when you feel tired, stressed, overcommitted, lonely, or unlovable. Starting over is an important step in meditation; it signifies your intention to be present and mindful. Intentions, as you will discover in later chapters, are powerful ingredients in the process of mind training.

Although we present mindful meditation as activities, we believe it is important to understand that mindful meditation is a way of life and not just a technique. It is a way of living with focused awareness in the present moment and is a vital step in developing a clear vision of reality. Daily practice of these exercises will help you to become present, awake, and aware. They will empower you to control your life and how you respond to suffering. When thoughts come into your mind, you learn to simply notice them and choose how to be present with them in a wakeful fashion. Just because you have a thought or a feeling doesn't mean that it gets to choose how to exist in your mind. *You* decide; you choose how to respond. You choose to be awake and present.

This wakefulness, or presence, will be felt not only by you; others will experience you as being more fully alive and attractive. We all notice and are attracted to people who are present, aware, and awake. As you begin to wake up, negative feelings such as dissatisfaction, loneliness, and sadness will diminish and lose their hold on you as you realize your ability to choose how to act. You will begin to notice the stuff of life and the impermanence of feelings in general. You will realize that you have even more choice about how to react. Your life will become more purposeful.

As your life becomes more purposeful, you will notice the consequences of your thoughts, feelings, and actions. You will make fewer mistakes and have fewer regrets. You will see others in a different way. Ultimately, if they are aware and present, they will see you in a different way as well.

Mindful meditation, or simply doing one thing at a time on purpose, will teach you how to accept uncomfortable physical sensations and emotions and just be with them as you reprogram your mind away from the monkey mind or habitual reactivity. Many people, just like us, report life-changing insights from mindful meditation.

Perhaps the most important insight that can occur with the practice of mindful meditation is the impermanent nature of life itself. The good, the bad, and the ugly are all transient. This concept is important as you explore more deeply the association of suffering and loneliness.

Suffering and Loneliness

"It has been a huge change for me to learn to be with my suffering rather than trying to make it go away or disappear," says Jon. "I used to judge my success on my earnings, cars, appearance, athletic prowess, and achievements. I was constantly comparing myself to others who were more successful, and I was always driven to do more. Slowly, I have learned to judge myself by whether I am being the person I want to be and living by my values, not calculating the value of my possessions or accomplishments. Finally, I am living in the real world rather an artificial one of my creation. I am having a real connection with the world irrespective of my material productivity and whether the sun is shining or storm clouds are rolling in. I have learned a new way to become aware of all of life's experiences and to respond in a more personally satisfying way.

"The challenge for me," he notes, "has been to give up many of my defenses. Previously, my self-talk used judging, blaming, rationalizing, denying, and every other defense mechanism. I began to consciously choose my actions and am no longer on automatic pilot, responding in a reactive manner. I have begun to learn how to be with suffering, pain, and resistance. I now just have dukkha and not the double dukkha that occurs when a painful experience is accompanied by a painful response. I understand that suffering in loneliness is an opportunity to practice and not a sign of failure. I can see loneliness for what it is and no longer need to run away or to identify with it."

Both of us have found that the following formula helps us to understand the importance of awareness and our reactions: Loneliness = Event x Reaction.

That is, loneliness is equal to an event that happens to you multiplied by your reaction to the event. If you are alone on a Saturday night and you react by being angry at your ex or feeling sorry for yourself, then your loneliness is going to multiply, and you will feel depressed, resentful, and sad.

However, if you are alone on a Saturday night and you simply notice it without judgment, it will pass and you'll feel fine. If you are alone on a Saturday night and you notice your loneliness and then focus on your breath, you will see how your reaction can dissolve the feeling of loneliness.

Here is another helpful formula: Suffering = Pain × Reaction.

Suffering is composed of the pain you feel multiplied by your reaction to the pain. Just as pain does not create suffering, events do not create loneliness. Whether we are lonely or simply alone depends on our reactions. There is no question that there is pain, and there is no question that there is loneliness. Humans are resilient and can handle both. It is our attachment to our beliefs about a particular outcome that determines how great the loneliness and suffering will be. If we are attached to a certain outcome or cling to an unrealistic expectation, then life will include more suffering. Our reactions multiply the amounts of pain and loneliness and even move them into the realm of pathology. Life is lonely at times; accept the loneliness as dukkha and do not add to it.

According to psychologist Martin Seligman, the formula for happiness is as follows: Happiness = S + C + V, in which S is "set range," or what you've inherited; C is the circumstances of your life; and V is the factors under your voluntary control—your reactions. Thus, happiness is formed by your inherited traits plus the circumstances of your life and how you react to those circumstances.

This is what we have learned about loneliness. Some things we have to accept (heredity), and some things we can change (circumstances and our reactions).

Most people struggle with loneliness by working hard to remove the external events that might have led to the loneliness. We acknowledge that this is a good idea, and we will talk about ways to do this later in the book. A problem occurs, however, when you believe that this is *all* you need to do to end loneliness. We have discovered that the way you react to loneliness—that is, your attachment to your beliefs about loneliness and how it affects your life or defines you and your life—is the ultimate key to never being lonely again.

Part Two

The Core of Loneliness in Five Questions

O nce we got over our ignorance—that is, quit ignoring the obvious —that we were creating loneliness by being attached to the wrong things, we started examining our lives piece by piece. To what were we attached? An image of ourselves? Other people? Our community? Our jobs? Doing something meaningful? And how did the attachment cause suffering and loneliness?

This is the personal work that was happening during the three years we avoided writing the original book. When we finally became more honest about the loneliness and began sharing with each other how we were making our way back from loneliness, some pieces came together. We want to share those pieces with you in this section of the book. We offer these five not-so-easy pieces in the form of questions, because it was in answering these questions that we clearly saw how we were creating loneliness—and how to never be lonely again.

3

Who Am I?

AT THE INNERMOST CORE OF ALL
LONELINESS IS A DEEP AND POWERFUL YEARNING
FOR UNION WITH ONE'S LOST SELF.

—Brendan Francis,
Irish poet, novelist, playwright

Our excitement about seeing the Dalai Lama, along with jet lag, was impacting the further reaches of Jon's brain. Because Pat's carefully packed suitcase had been lost by the airlines, she was wondering what she was going to wear when she saw one of the world's most revered people. In the process of talking with Pat, Jon began to wonder what he should wear. A discussion ensued, and he and his friend Addison decided to go to an Indian clothing store and see what they could find in Delhi before heading to Dharamasala.

Jon's Lesson:
Do the Clothes Make the Man?

Addison and I took a motorized rickshaw for a long, long ride that left us approximately three blocks from where we began (nothing is easy in India). We entered a bazaar that was rumored to have the best selection of Indian apparel, and the rickshaw driver delivered us to a

specific salesman, who greeted us like long-lost relatives while he ushered us down to a basement room filled with lavish oriental rugs.
There he introduced us to another gentleman, seated on a grand over-
stuffed sofa, who was pouring tea for three. We told him that we were
here for clothes, not rugs, but he assured us that the friendly way to do
business in India was to first have tea and get acquainted. Reluctantly,
we sat down.

After twenty minutes of repeating the fact that we weren't there to
buy a rug, even though we had no doubt his rugs were the finest in
India, we were able to extricate ourselves only by announcing that we
were in his country for the specific purpose of meeting with a very
important person and that for this occasion we wanted to look regal.
With this pronouncement, another gentleman magically appeared who
just coincidentally happened to have received a brand-new shipment of
clothing that would be precisely what is called for on such an occasion.

Taking a serpentine route through various Indian statues, silk
scarves, and other tchotchkes, we arrived at the men's clothing bou-
tique. The salesman grinned as he sized me up, both literally and figuratively. He went through the motions with his tape measure, but I
had the uncanny feeling that he was thinking, *No way is this bozo going
to look like an Indian!*

He walked behind a curtained doorway and returned first with a
beautiful turban and a Bollywood-style Indo-Western suit with a
matching pair of *mojari* shoes. He said this would be perfect. I put on
the clothes and thought that I looked like the Indian version of Lady
Gaga. I suggested that maybe we try something different, maybe a
little less elegant. He said, "How about a high-class *sherwani*, [a long
coatlike garment]?" I thought that also might be over the top. Forty-
five minutes and several outfits later, I was having him box up a nice-
looking striped *kurta* top with a plain pair of drawstring pants. I
thought that these were just about perfect for meeting royalty, and
they had cost me only two and a half times the amount of money I was

hoping to spend. Later, however, I learned from the hotel clerk that they were actually pajamas.

This was just one of many lessons I learned in India, and it was not the last time I'd have to look at my attachments and the images I cling to. Am I attached to being what others want me to be? Do I cling to the idea of always being perfect? Am I a Westerner who is trying to be an Easterner? Who am I? On my shopping venture, I was trying to be someone I wasn't (i.e., a well-dressed Indian) to impress others. The whole experience felt surreal—like Halloween or a masquerade. I also felt driven to do the right thing according to Western protocol. I remembered the Latin phrase *Vestis virum facit*, "Clothes make the man," and concluded that this was a proper thought. Meanwhile, my fellow travelers were following similar calls and selecting what they considered the garb that would please His Holiness.

Later, back at the hotel, we checked in with our guide, Jhampa, to find out exactly what was the appropriate dress for meeting His Holiness. He laughed and said that His Holiness wants Westerners to look like Westerners. In other words, he thought that we should be ourselves and that there was no set protocol as long as we were comfortable. What was important was to simply be yourself; be real and not phony.

Encouragement to be real is not a new thing to me. After all, I was a product of the late 1960s and early 1970s, and that was our mantra: "Be real, man." Hearing Jhampa's words was like déjà vu. What has happened to me? Have I been asleep for thirty-five years? I seem to have lost touch with, sight of, or connection to my essence. I struggle with what is real. Who am I? Really, who am I? When I concentrate on answering that question I think that I am a husband, a father, a professor, a psychologist, a friend, an athlete, and an author. I'm attached to these roles; I've invested a lot in them.

But when I strip away the clothes and the outward appearance, the many letters behind my name, my numerous accomplishments, the roles I play, and the other signs of social status, who am I? Am I the person I say I am? Am I the person I really want to be? What is really important to me? Do I need to hide behind clothes, titles, possessions, and accomplishments?

I have worked very hard to accomplish so many goals. Few people have published, traveled, or produced as much, yet I feel like the Mark Twain quote "Having lost sight of our goals, we redouble our efforts." Have I been working so hard because I don't know who I am?

So where am I going and what am I doing? There's a sign on the wall of the coffee shop I frequent that quotes Indian philosopher Rabindranath Tagore (1861–1941), "Our task is not to increase property, but to be." Have I merely been acquiring material goods and symbols of status?

I decide to focus on my breathing and return to my source of comfort, so I pick up a Buddhist book. I open to a page with a quote from the Digha Nikaya ("Long Discourses"): "A serpent regularly sheds it skin: similarly we too have to let go of wrong attitudes and desires. Our lives are characterized by change and transformation; we have to adapt to new situations constantly. This is how we get freedom and happiness in life."

India taught me that one of the core causes of suffering, which in my case was loneliness, is the alienation you have from your self. I was lonely because I was hiding my true self from myself. As we will discuss in this chapter, the desire to look outside ourselves to define ourselves creates suffering and loneliness. As we cling to the roles we play or to a false image of ourselves, we move further into loneliness, for how can someone know us if we don't know ourselves? How can you and I make contact when I don't know who I am?

Know Thyself

Only through recognizing that loneliness begins with the alienation from self can we build a bridge back to connection—first with ourselves and then with others. It is pretty easy to see that trying to be someone you are not can create suffering. Talk about setting yourself up for failure. But trying to be someone you are not can also create loneliness because it generates uncertainty and anxiety in you and in those who come in contact with you. You know what it's like to be around someone who is a fake, who pretends to be kind but isn't, who claims to be your friend but doesn't act friendly.

You have to know who you are and act congruently to be available for connection. More important, you have to know who you are and be faithful to yourself to even know that you exist. If you keep changing your image to satisfy others, aren't you just being a mirror image of one person after another? Aren't you living their lives, not your life? Basic comfort comes from knowing who you are and acting accordingly. First and foremost, don't hide from yourself. Be available, be present, be mindful.

Socrates said, "The unexamined life is not worth living," and we know for sure that an unexamined life can leave you disappointed as well as lonely. You can actually be lonely for your true self. This point is usually easier to see in others than in oneself. An unexamined life is evident to you in the people you've met who seem clueless about their values or what they stand for. They tend to flail about in life without direction, shifting from one activity to another, hoping something will grab and hold their interest. Oblivious to the effect they have on others, they may be rude, unkind, or simply insensitive. You've no doubt been embarrassed by their unconscious behavior. They may even mean well and overcompensate or overfunction—that is, do too much and make others uncomfortable by overdoing. They don't know who they are.

The alienation from self creates a hole in your life, a vacuum of sorts, and nature abhors a vacuum. Remember that loneliness is a drive; loneliness for your true self can drive you to seek your identity in a relationship, a job, or even in the clothes you wear. Loneliness for your true self can make material goods far too important; you become identified with the car you drive, the watch you wear, or the latest gadget you own. The opposite can also be true: you become identified with the car, the watch, or the gadget that you *don't* have. Looking outside yourself to know who you are is a dead-end street that ends in loneliness.

The alienation from self creates a particular brand of loneliness that will be alleviated only by examining your life in a mindful way. This means determining who you are and what you stand for. If you've ever spent much time with someone who just can't be consistent, who makes a promise but doesn't follow through, you understand what it's like trying to relate to someone who doesn't know who he is. In contrast, it's refreshing to be in contact with someone who shows up consistently and confidently, time after time. You come to trust and develop a regard for this person. You get the sense that she knows who she is and that you can count on her.

The alienation from self leads to a lack of trust and a disconnection between you and others, but the surprising fact about this type of loneliness is that it starts within. It is an internal process that then infiltrates our relationships. Knowing who you are is the beginning of the end of loneliness.

Before we go any further, we are going to ask you to answer the question "Who am I?"

Exercise 8: Who Am I?

Jot down, off the top of your head, at least three or four clear answers to this question. It will be interesting to see if your answers change as you read further. You may either write free-form, letting the ideas flow, or just list some words or phrases that describe you.

1. _____
2. _____
3. _____
4. _____

Did you answer the question? The remainder of this chapter, as well as the rest of the book, will have a lot more impact if you take concrete action and get involved by doing the exercises and not skipping over them. To realize our promise that you will never be lonely again, you have to provide your personal details to complete the protocols.

Here are some answers we've received from people who have completed this exercise:

Wife
Husband
Mother
Father
Friend
Grandmother
I am Sara.
I am reserved.
I am conservative and realistic.
I am psychic.
I am a spirit on the earth.
I am a child of God.

It's not uncommon for the question "Who am I?" to create resistance and even anxiety, because it puts you on the spot. We asked you to first answer the question off the top of your head in order to take the pressure off and start the process of self-examination. Many of the answers listed above were given off the cuff and could easily change with more time for thought, which we will provide for you in subsequent sections. The question contains some crazy wisdom, because embedded in the query is a request for a promise and a commitment.

For example, if you wrote "I am a loving person," this would imply that you exemplify love in the way you live your life. However, if you are like many of us, you can think of times when you acted in ways that would not be described as loving. This inconsistency creates dissonance and guilt. But guilt can lead you to integrity; it reminds you to get back on track, to get your behavior in line with your core values[2] and the person you want to be. Who you are and whom you want to be is the guiding force for your life. Your decisions, your relationships, and your next move are in direct response to the person you believe you are, and this belief can guide you toward or away from loneliness.

---

[2] Steven Stosny, Ph.D., *Building Core Value, Science of the Soul,* compassionpower.com

Depending on how you answer the question of who you are, your responses may or may not serve as a guiding force away from loneliness. If your answers look like some of those listed above—that is, a series of roles you fill, like husband, wife, partner, or friend—these can give you a modicum of guidance, for they assume certain functions to which you may ascribe, but you are not simply reduced to those roles. Your identity is bigger than that, and it, not a role, is your guiding force. If you listed "grandmother" as an answer, this may provide you with direction in making decisions about your grandchildren (and perhaps other relationships), but it doesn't tell you what to do or how to act on a moment-to-moment basis. We are going to ask you to go deeper, to be more mindful, as you continue to ponder the question of who you are. Let's look to the Four Noble Truths for some direction.

The Second Noble Truth is that the origin of suffering is attachment to transient things. When you base your identity on impermanent conditions, you set yourself up for suffering, alienation from self, and a longing for your true self. The roles we play come and go over time. Political and even religious beliefs change with new experiences or information. The status or power we hold can tumble when the economic wind changes direction. Cars rust, watches stop ticking, relationships change, beauty wanes, jobs are outsourced, fame fades, friends and family members die, health declines, information becomes irrelevant, and gadgets break and must be replaced. Impermanence is the natural order of the universe. Clinging to an image of yourself that is dependent on impermanent things creates suffering as well as loneliness for a stable sense of self. Based on this knowledge, we ask you to complete the exercise again with different instructions and a more mindful approach.

Exercise 9: **Who Am I, Really?**

This time around, think about the essential traits that make you *you*. For example, consider how you want others to see you: how you want your loved ones to experience you and how you want to be remembered after you die. When others speak of you, what do you want them to say? What kind of person do you aspire to be? What would you like your eulogy to say? In addition, how do you *want* to behave? What do you stand for? What attributes do you want to be the driving force of your life?

1. _____
2. _____
3. _____
4. _____

When we work with clients, individuals and couples alike, we ask them to answer this question early in the session, before the tougher issues arise. Then when an issue comes up that meets with resistance, we use the answers as a guiding force. For example, if Jenny answers that she is loving, kind, supportive, and dependable, then in a session in which Jenny says that she doesn't want to invite John's mother to the wedding, we can look back at Jenny's answers and say, "Jenny, what would a loving person do? What would a kind person do?"

Of course, the most common response is "Well, why should I be loving when his mother hasn't been loving to me?" Our answer is "Because you are in charge of the kind of person you want to be. Besides, you feel better about yourself when you do the right thing. Don't let someone else (such as John's mother) decide how you are going to feel about yourself or decide what kind of person you are going to be. Don't let someone else pull you away from your true self. Don't let someone else decide your core values."

We might add, "Don't let life events pull you away from your core values. Life is suffering, remember? It doesn't always go as planned. Don't get attached to impermanent things."

Pat's Lesson: Who Am I in India?

India gave us so many opportunities to ask "Who am I?" There's nothing like international travel to bring out the best—and the worst—in people. As mentioned earlier, unlike Jon, I traveled east to get to India: from Austin to Atlanta, then to Paris, and from there to Delhi. The flight from Austin to Atlanta was uneventful, and the flight from Atlanta to Paris seemed normal at the time; only later did I learn that my bags stayed in Paris for an extra ten days.

It was at Charles de Gaulle Airport in Paris that the challenges began. Due to some glitch, all the passengers who disembarked from the Atlanta flight were left stranded at the airport for four hours, standing in two narrow hallways connected by an escalator. People were crammed together with no room to sit or move. Unless you were at the front of the line, you couldn't see what the trouble was. At first people stood patiently, half asleep (it was in the middle of the night), but after a while their patience started to grow thin. There was no food, no water, no bathroom, and no information. What an opportunity to ask "Who am I?" Fortunately, a friend had warned me, "The trip to India begins when you leave home; the lessons you will learn will begin long before you think."

Imagine for a moment that you are in this situation. How do you think you would handle it? What kind of person are you in a situation in which life doesn't go as you planned? Most of us, on a good day, when life is predictable, can act in a pretty decent manner, but what are you like on a bad day, when life doesn't go your way? Tough times afford the opportunity to answer "Who am I?" with conviction, not just conjecture.

By the time the flight left Paris for Delhi, it was eight hours behind schedule. Jhampa had arranged for all the tour members to be greeted at the airport by a group of Tibetan monks led by a man named Tenzin (we would meet many Tenzins; they are named after the current Dalai Lama, Tenzin Gyatso). Tenzin was scheduled to pick me up at 8:00 PM at the airport in Delhi and take me to the restaurant to join the rest of the group.

With the delay, however, the 8:00 PM arrival ended up being a 4:00 AM arrival. I had no clue how I was going to find the rest of the group. The thought of making my way alone through Delhi in the early morning hours was quite disconcerting, to say the least. I was incredibly nervous when I got off that plane, so you can imagine my relief when I saw not only Tenzin but another six smiling monks in their maroon robes waiting for me and waving as if I were their long-lost friend.

Looking back at this incident, I realize that of course Tenzin would have been tracking the flight from Paris; of course he would have known that my plane was delayed. Nevertheless, there is a part of me that would answer "Who am I?" with "I am a person who doesn't believe that others will be there for me; I am alone in this world." Today I know that this isn't accurate, but old messages die hard, and they easily come back to life under stress. To change this internal perception, I first had to know that it existed.

Facing Your Perceptions of Yourself

Do you have similar perceptions of yourself? When asked who you are, do you, if you are being honest, admit any of the following?

I am a person who doubts the love and care of others.

I am a person without support.

I am difficult to love.

I am hard to get along with.

I am demanding.

I am the only one I can rely on. I am destined to be alone.

I don't have time for fun.

Let us explain why this is important. Let's say that you, like Pat, have a belief that others aren't there to help you or that if anything is going to get done right, you have to do it yourself. What would it be like to live with someone (i.e., like yourself) who won't accept help, who doesn't believe you when you say you want to help, who shuts you out and does everything alone, leaving you no way to show that you care? What would it be like being in a relationship with someone who ultimately believes that he or she can do everything better than you?

The internal beliefs that you harbor about yourself, which might stem from your history, influence the behavior and the attitudes of others. At this point in life, it doesn't matter how the messages got in your head; it's what you do about these messages that is important. One of our favorite quotes from psychologist Albert Ellis is "The best years of your life are the ones in which you decide your problems are your own. You do not blame them on your mother, the ecology, or the president. You realize that you control your own destiny." The field of self-help has spent far too much time and effort finding fault with the people in our past. This is *your* life; however you got here, where you go from here is up to you.

Part of knowing yourself is facing the dark side of your character. We all have unbecoming traits. The way to move on from these traits is to acknowledge that they exist and then replace them with traits that represent your core values.

How do you change your mind? How do you change the negative messages that have been in your brain for ages?

First, acknowledge the message; for example, "I am difficult to love." Second, amend the message to reflect your goal; "I am lovable." Third, act on it; ask yourself what lovable people do and then do that over and over until you no longer deny you are lovable. The ingrained message won't change until your actions and your behaviors change.

The Regretful Person

As we interviewed people for this book and asked "Who are you?" we sometimes heard a litany of regrets for past deeds and actions. The regret wasn't always immediately obvious in our early conversations, but as we spent more time talking and the topics became more intimate, we began to hear statements like "I am a person who left his son at an early age," "I haven't been a good father," or "I was a terrible wife and stepmother." One young man said, "I put my parents through hell, and now my mom is dead and I can never make up for it." A woman in her sixties said, "I was unfaithful—more than once; I live with that guilt." More often than you might think, some of these people spoke of loneliness as a penance of sorts: "I deserve to be lonely," "I created this situation myself," or "I'm ashamed of myself."

The question is what to do with your regrets. The query itself brings up your personal philosophy of life. Many people say, "I don't believe in regret; I have no regrets. All my actions have been leading up to today and have made me the person I am, and I'm fine with that person." Others say, "I did the best I could at that time; it's not the best

I can do today, but that was then and this is now." Still others feel a sense of guilt or remorse for their past deeds and welcome an opportunity to be free of these feelings.

Guilt occurs when your actions do not line up with your core values. If your core value is to be a faithful wife and you are not faithful, you will feel guilty. This guilt, by the way, is a sign of mental health. People who have no sense of guilt have no moral compass and ultimately cannot be trusted. Guilt is corrective; it is designed to bring you back to your core values.

So what can you do with the past deeds about which you feel regret, remorse, or guilt? First, let the feelings guide you back to your core value. In the example of infidelity, you would ask yourself, "What would a faithful wife do? How can I demonstrate my fidelity?" Then do it over and over, until your behavior lines up with your core values and the person you want to be.

Sometimes an apology, amends, penance, or reparation is required to reinforce your core values. If you are like the son mentioned above who cannot apologize to his deceased mother—at least in person—you may need to "pay it forward." In other words, perform acts of kindness for other people, but in your mother's memory. You might also ask yourself, "What is required for me to forgive myself and release my guilt?" Surely acts of service or compassion are more powerful than a life sentence of loneliness, and if you are capable of compassion, do the recipients of your compassion include you?

The Depressed Person

Other people we interviewed referred to depression when answering "Who am I?" We heard statements like "I'm depressed" or "I've been depressed for a long time." Clinical depression, which can have a multitude of causes including biology, genetics, environmental stress as well as lifestyle, is a serious mental health condition. Fortunately, with today's treatment approaches, no one has to suffer from this disorder, which leads 10 percent of those most seriously burdened and untreated to attempt suicide. The symptoms of clinical depression include excessive crying or sadness; extreme mood swings; erratic behavior; loss of interest in friends, loved ones, or any type of pleasure; loss of appetite; weight gain or loss; anger; irritability; fatigue; changes in sleep habits (too much or too little); consistent negative thinking; anxiety; paranoia; exhaustion; forgetfulness; and a sense of foreboding. If you have questions about your own symptoms, do not hesitate to seek help. Relief is readily available.

Situational depression, unlike clinical depression, is caused by life events and the way that one views and reacts to these events. Situational depression can be exacerbated by being attached to the wrong things and being out of touch with your true self. Pat can tell you firsthand about the stress and heartache of being out of touch with yourself.

"For much of my life," she explains, "when I felt depressed it was because I was living my life according to someone else's standards and not my own. I tried to be what others wanted me to be in order to ward off my deep experience of loneliness. I was so out of touch with my own core values that much of the time I was dissociated, clueless about my feelings and without any self-knowledge. I was like a ship without a rudder, blown about by any passing wind. I was looking outward to others to heal my loneliness when all the time I needed to look inward because I was lonely for my true self."

Like being attached to regrets, being attached to grief and sadness can keep you from knowing who you truly are and can build a wall of loneliness between you and others. You become stuck, without direction, and without motivation. Because the alienation from self can have dire consequences, we encourage you to act in earnest when you answer the question "Who am I?" This inquiry has more power than you might think to make sure that you are never lonely again.

The Negative Person

It is possible to create a negative internal state by harboring discouraging beliefs about yourself, others, or the world around you. You don't have to look far to find some bad news or to recall a depressing event from your history, but dwelling on it will not improve the situation—in fact, it will make it worse. The most efficient way to eliminate negative thinking is to replace it with positive thinking, which you reinforce with positive action. Acting out your core values every day and remembering the positive thoughts and feelings that accompany the positive actions is vital. Do not let a day go by without a visible action that represents your core values. One new action can change your life for the better in just a short time.

Exercise 10: **Moving Through Pain**

Because regret, depression, and negativity can be debilitating, we want to offer you some immediate relief through this exercise. The process can be used for most any experience or strong sensation. We ask that you choose one painful feeling at a time to focus on. You might want to mark this page so you can refer back to it if and when strong emotions come up while you're reading the rest of this book. There's nothing like a real-life application of principles to make you believe that you really can reach a state in which you will never be lonely again.

Begin by getting in touch with your body and your breath. Sit comfortably in an upright position so your breathing is free and unencumbered. Take the time you need to focus on your breath, feeling the air come into your body and go out of your body. With each exhalation, relax and let go of any tension. If thoughts enter your mind, simply watch them flow by like a boat floating downstream. Once these thoughts float away you can consciously move your thoughts back to the breath.

As you continue to relax and be aware of your breathing, let your mind move to a place in your body where you feel pain. Know that the pain is there; move toward it. Feel it in your body. See what scene emerges before you as you feel the pain. Hear the sounds of this pain. Taste the taste and smell the smells and feel what it is like to visit this pain. Focus on where it lives in your body. Give it a color and a form. Make it larger and brighter. Comfort yourself in knowing that you can watch this pain flow down the river if you wish. Stay with it for a moment.

Now, as you watch the pain, imagine that someone close to you has experienced this very same pain. Just let this person appear in your mind. Don't question the person who appears, simply let yourself be curious and concerned about that person's pain and what it might be like. Let your mind recognize that the same pain you have felt now lives in this person. Notice the person's familiar body posture and facial expression. Acknowledge that you share this common experience.

Feel the pain that the other person is feeling. Now take on that pain and join it with yours. Imagine that you are bearing the burden for this person as well as for many others. Notice and feel others' burdens lift as you share their suffering. See the relief as they realize that they do not suffer alone. Feel your own sense of relief as you honor the experience of shared pain.

Now decide where you want the pain to go. Shall it move to compassion, to a deeper understanding of others' pain? Shall it simply float down the river and join the past? Shall it move you to be kinder to yourself and others? Shall it remind you to be truer to yourself and your core values? Remind yourself of who you are and who you plan to be. Change your experience in a comforting way as you focus on your breath—in and out, relaxing and supporting—and then come back to your current awareness refreshed and renewed.

Knowing Who You Are

Because self-knowledge—or the lack of it—guides your decision making, knowing yourself and being clear about the kind of person you want to be affects every waking moment. What you are doing right now is a reflection of who you are. Maybe reading this book says that you are a lifelong learner or are interested in improving your life. You may be someone who has shared our experiences of loneliness. It is very important to keep in mind that who you are right now may not reflect whom you would like to be. You may be lonely at this moment, and that certainly isn't a life goal or a state to which you aspire. Knowing who you are in terms of your guiding principles and your core values can begin with an honest analysis of where you have been, where you are now, and where you want to be in the future.

Exercise 11: **Do I Know Myself?**

This meditation is designed to help you discover your experience of loneliness as a result of being disconnected from yourself. It is hard to be connected if you do not know who you are, who you *really* are. This meditation requires persistence and the willingness to challenge or push your comfort level.

Begin by focusing on your breathing and letting yourself relax. With each breath, notice the calmness and comfort that you feel. When you are ready, ask yourself "Who am I?" and respond to your answer with "Yes, but who am I, really?"

Ask yourself this over and over each day for at least ten days, allowing thirty minutes each day. When roles like parent, sibling, and friend come up, reply with "That is just a role I play; who am I really?" If you respond with a state of being, such as being lonely or happy, say, "That is just a state of being; who am I really?" Respond to every answer—whether it be a name, a label, a memory, or an interpretation—in the same fashion.

Intimate and accurate self-knowledge is the key to fulfillment as well as to a life of connection rather than alienation. Much of life's discontent and misery comes from acting in ways that go against the person you would like to be or from behaving in a manner that does not reflect your core values, the principles by which you want to live. The first step in knowing yourself is to clarify who you are and whom you want to be.

Exercise 12: **What Is Important to Me?**

In this activity, we ask you to identify the five items that are your most important possessions. Think of anything, large or small. It could be your home, a new car, your grandfather's watch, a special plant, or your antique footstool. List the five items:

1. _____
2. _____
3. _____
4. _____
5. _____

Now we would like you to carefully comment, after each one, why each item is important to you. Psychologists call this a projective device, because all of us project ourselves onto objects and invest them with a comfort or a value that others probably don't share. What are the common themes about you and the objects you have chosen? You may use this exercise to refine your thinking as you answer "Who am I?"

If you claim to be a loving person in answer to "Who am I?" then you should have numerous examples of loving gestures, and the people who know you should have even more examples. Living life in line with what you stand for evokes confidence and makes you feel connected to yourself. This can be the good news, or this can be the bad news. If, on the one hand, you truly believe you are a good and worthy person and that your everyday actions corroborate this perception, then you will feel calm and congruent. If, on the other hand, you believe that you are a worthwhile person but you let others treat you as if you were not worthy or valuable, then you will feel anxious, incongruent, and at odds with yourself. Eventually, something has to give. The first step in knowing yourself is to put your behaviors in line with who you are.

No matter how many friends you have or how successful you are at work or play, if you are not living a life that reflects your internal values, commitments, and perceptions, a sense of loneliness will haunt you. When your everyday life is not a reflection of your internal character, you develop a low regard for yourself and are inclined to project that onto others. When you don't think much of yourself, it's easy to imagine that others feel the same way about you. How do you act toward someone who you think doesn't like you? Are you anxious? Angry? Avoidant? How do you relate to someone who you believe has a low opinion of you? Are you defensive? Demanding? Defiant?

These behaviors will, of course, increase the likelihood that you will have difficulty making a connection. Who wants to befriend an angry person? Who wants to get closer to someone who is demanding or defensive? Worse yet, if your perception of yourself is negative, you can unwittingly seek out people and situations that will validate your viewpoint. Incongruence—living a life that lies about who you really are—is a primary source of loneliness. This is why knowing who you are is the first step toward a guarantee that you will never be lonely again.

Exercise 13: **A Situation of Concern**

Lest you think you've heard this all before and that our approach is a collection of clichés, we're going to challenge you right up front with a real-life experiment with which you can experience the power of this book. First, begin by thinking of an issue in your present life that is causing you concern: something you are worried about, something that you believe creates your loneliness, a relationship that's a cause of disappointment or conflict, a situation you've been avoiding, or something that requires you to take action, even if the action is simply the way you think. Make a note of it. Write it down and define it clearly.

"A situation of concern in my life now is . . ."

Now that you have defined the situation of concern, look back at your answers to "Who Am I?" and "Who Am I, Really?" This is your resource bank. Use any answers that apply by asking yourself the following: What would this kind of person do in response to the situation of concern?

For example, here are some of the responses we've received as concerns:

I have no companion.
Will my company make it in this economy?
How do I fulfill the role of grandmother to my stepchildren's children?
Growing older.

If one of these concerns mirrors one of yours, you might look at your answers for guidance. For example, see if your list contains anything like the following:

I am a loving person.
I am creative.
I am supportive.
I am a person of integrity.

Look for the resources that fit best. If you have no companion, you might ask, "What would a supportive person do in this situation?" Do you know anyone else who doesn't have a companion? You probably do, given the fact that close to half the adult population is single. What would a supportive person who doesn't have a companion do if that were a concern? How could support be used to address this concern? Supportive people rarely lack companionship. What would constitute an act of support that would take some effort but leave no doubt that you were being supportive?

If you hear yourself saying, "I've done that and it didn't work," then most likely you have just done what is easy. Taking the easy way out—for example, being supportive to a colleague at work whom you've supported before or being supportive to someone who has been kind to you in the past—won't change you or move the ball forward in warding off loneliness. You have to do the *most difficult* right thing. Doing what's easy usually means that you've done it before, and it won't have a lasting effect on your psyche. You have to give your psyche a power jolt. Think of a supportive act that not only is timely but also takes your breath away at the thought of it! It has to be correct and appropriate but challenging.

Following this line of thinking, and using the two lists, you might ask the following: What would a creative person do about his or her company in a tough economy? How would a person of integrity handle growing older? How would a loving person manage being a grandmother to her stepgrandchildren? Once you have your answer, do it!

Finally, let's say that a core value of yours is being helpful. Once a day you should make it a point to help someone. It may be assisting a stranger, sending a text message to your cousin who has been having a computer problem, or running an errand to save your partner time. Whatever you do, you must do it for the intrinsic value of helping, not for getting accolades or appreciation in return. If you give only to get, you are simply bartering, not helping. Even worse, if you give to get, it feels manipulative, not helpful. Few of us want a core value that includes manipulation.

The loneliness caused by being alienated from yourself is eradicated only when your behavior is in line with the very best person you want to be. The calm that comes with congruence will enable you to move on to the next four questions and be one step closer to never being lonely again.

4

Am I Connected?

AS WE GROW UP WE ATTACH LESS IMPORTANCE TO AFFECTION,
FRIENDSHIP, AND MUTUAL SUPPORT. INSTEAD WE EMPHASIZE RACE,
RELIGION, OR NATIONALITY. WE FORGET THE MAIN THING
AND CONCENTRATE ON THE MOST TRIVIAL.

—The Dalai Lama

When 9/11 happened, whom did you call first? Who were the people you wanted near you or wanted to make sure were safe? Whose voice did you want to hear? Who were the people you wanted to contact immediately, without thinking? Perhaps you were one of millions who were watching the morning news and actually saw the second plane fly into the World Trade Center as it happened. If so, what did you do first? Who were the people you reached out to, and who contacted you?

The chances are that these are the people to whom you were most connected at the time. Tragedy, loss, and threats to survival bring out our ties of connection. Are these same people in your life now? If a tragedy were to occur today, whom would you call? If you hear of a severe weather threat, whom do you want with you in your storm shelter? In contrast, if you receive great news, who are the people you want to celebrate with you?

71

Going through life alone isn't nearly as much fun or as comforting. It's plain to see that we need human connection to survive when we are infants; what's not always plain to see is that we need human connection to thrive as adults—and the connection has to be meaningful. Superficial niceties are not enough. Contact has to be personal as well as purposeful to be potent.

One of our favorite stories about purposeful connection is from the Dalai Lama; he shared it during a public lecture several years ago. The incident took place when he was on a speaking tour and was staying in the hotel where the event was held. While on a break from his presentation, he received heartbreaking news from his homeland, Tibet. Then, as now, his life was dedicated to negotiating a peaceful solution to the Chinese occupation of Tibet, which has resulted in an elimination of all signs of independent Tibetan culture: history, language, religion, artifacts, agriculture, natural resources, and not to mention countless lives.

During this particular speaking event, word came to His Holiness that his latest efforts had once again failed, and his beloved Tibet was still in jeopardy of annihilation. The news caused a deep sadness to come over him, and he retreated to his room in despair. As fortune would have it, the hotel maid was cleaning his room just at that moment, so he began to talk to her about his sorrow and grief. After he had talked and she had listened, he began to feel better, and his despair lifted. The point of the story, as he related it, was that the simple act of human comfort and connection enabled him to regain his composure and continue his lecture with a lighter heart.

Without understanding the importance of human connection, one might be tempted to ask how a Nobel prizewinning, god-king of international renown could be comforted by a hotel maid. The answer is simple: connection knows no status, gender, or age. Connection, especially when it comes in the form of compassion, is a powerful force no matter what the source.

One of the most important concepts in this book is that your most important resource is your capacity for connection and compassion. We all need contact; therefore your attention, your energy, and your interest are vital commodities. Compassion, which is simply the desire to ease suffering, is a healing force in the universe. You have that force within you. Your presence is a life-giving strength to others. You should know, either now or after reading this book, how very precious human contact truly is.

You can never tell when you might be called upon to be an important source of connection for even a stranger—or vice versa. In the quiet of that hotel room, the Dalai Lama shared, the woman listened, and they connected, and the connection helped to lift the sadness from his heart. There was no loneliness in that exchange.

The Art of Noticing

Inquiring minds can have a field day with this story. Did the maid know that he was the Dalai Lama? If so, how did she keep her composure? ("Yikes, I'm talking to the Dalai Lama!") Did His Holiness just sit down and start talking to her? Or did she simply notice his despair and begin a conversation?

The mere act of noticing others, and being aware, is powerful. Noticing is a key to connection, for it is the first step out of your own world and into the world of the other. Our friend Daniel, who went to India with us, experienced this firsthand the week before we had our audience with the Dalai Lama. During the days preceding our visit, the eight of us spent time exploring Dharamsala and its vicinity in northern India. Jhampa had arranged day trips to monasteries, a visit to a Buddhist library, hikes in the foothills of the Himalayas, and a special visit to the Tibetan Children's Village (TCV).

The TCV was conceptualized by His Holiness out of concern for the many children who were orphaned or left destitute by war, hunger, and/or the psychological devastation of losing their families and their homeland. The Chinese occupation of Tibet in 1959 led to the deaths of more than a million Tibetans and the flight of 100,000 refugees to India. Many of those who fled were children. Aided by two of his sisters and many caring individuals, His Holiness founded the TCV, which has grown throughout India. We were able to experience the success of one of the villages in an unforgettable way.

At the beginning of our visit to the village, we met formally with the headmistress, who talked to us about how the TCV was formed, as well as its goal and its purpose. We were given a tour of the grounds and then were invited to meet some of the children individually. Each of us was introduced to one child, which afforded an opportunity for dialogue and exchange because they all spoke English.

Daniel was paired with Ngawang, a six-year-old girl who had just come to the village because her father had been killed and her mother couldn't afford to feed her and her siblings. Daniel is a former NFL football player from the Green Bay Packers, and he looks every bit the part. He's a big guy with a heart to match. When he was introduced to Ngawang, he was told that her father had recently died, so when he sat down beside her, he simply noticed. He said, "I imagine that you are sad that your father died." At first Ngawang just nodded her head, but as Daniel kept noticing, just sitting quietly, she started to cry—softly at first and then with heavy sobs, as children do when they are shedding sorrow. She cried for quite some time, and all the while Daniel just noticed and cared and connected. They shared a compassionate exchange. Daniel, with his strong desire to ease Ngawang's suffering, used his presence as a source of comfort.

A cynic might say, "Well, Daniel just walked in and out of Ngawang's life; what good did that do?" The answer is that we don't really know. Daniel remembers that time with poignancy, but we don't know what the impact was on Ngawang; besides, the end of that story isn't written yet. Daniel is still in contact with Ngawang, but that's their story; let's get back to your story by asking you a question.

Think about someone in your life who simply noticed you: a person who cared enough, even for a moment, to pay attention, see you, and hear you in a way that made you feel important or cared for in some manner. Who was that person? Was it a parent or a grandparent, a teacher, a neighbor, a stranger, a friend, or a coach? What did he or she do? Why do you think you can still remember this? What impact did it have on your life? Take some time to ponder these questions.

People who consistently notice and act with compassion are never lonely. However, people who are unable or unwilling to get out of their own frame of reference—their own world, so to speak—find this to be a major detriment to connection. This explains why a lot of nice people are lonely. You can be busy doing for others and being pleasant, polite, and even thoughtful, but if there is no connection, no exchange between you and the other person beyond the superficial, it won't ward off loneliness. Perhaps this is best explained by correcting an old adage that most of us have been taught, the one that says you have to love yourself before you can love someone else. The truth is that this is backward.

"The American way is to first feel good about yourself and then feel good about others," notes Benedictine monk Thomas Keating, "but spiritual traditions say it's the other way around." Outer focus, not inner focus, is much closer to the path away from loneliness and toward happiness and mental health.

In our review of Western literature, we found that the subject of love basically boils down to the following: "Love is a response to getting your needs met" or "If you treat me the way I want to be treated, I love you." This what-have-you-done-for-me-lately attitude has no scientific research to back it up. If someone treats you the way you want to be treated, it may give you pleasure, but it doesn't create happiness. Pleasure is transitory; pleasure exhausts itself in the moment. You get pleasure from eating your favorite food, but it won't make you happy past the last mouthful.

Happiness and the cure for loneliness come from loving and caring. In fact, some scholars argue that the only love you can truly experience or feel is the *act* of loving. Even when someone touches you, loves you, or is kind to you, what you feel are your own feelings, loving back.

Crazy wisdom says that it is in loving others that you love yourself. It's the act of following your own core values, being the person that you say you want to be, that enables you to find yourself, experience yourself, and love yourself. Doing what is easy won't work.

Exercise 14: **Being Supportive**

Think about a relationship that is important to you but that has some distance, conflict, or disappointment. Now imagine having a conversation with this person in which you ask the following:

1. What is one thing I could do to be supportive of you? (Come up with an answer you might receive.)
2. What is another thing I could do to be supportive that would really help you as well as our relationship?
3. What, in your wildest imagination, could I do that would be supersupportive and over-the-top helpful to you and our relationship?

There are a couple of ways to use this exercise. The first way is to take it live. That is, really ask someone the three questions. However, don't ask unless you actually are willing to be generous. Once you get your answers, choose the one that is most difficult for you but that you can still give with generosity. Do the most difficult right thing: the act that might take your breath away at the thought of it but that you know would make a difference.

The second way to use the exercise is to imagine that you are the other person and answer the three questions from his or her point of view. Then act on your own intuition and volition. Again, the point is to do the most difficult right thing.

Finally, think about the answer to the third question. Does it create resistance in you? If so, the greater the resistance, the more you might want to explore this option, for sometimes connection requires that you do the very act that you resist the most.

Get Outside Yourself

The next time you leave your home, make it a point to look someone in the eye and smile and say hello. It could be the checkout person at the grocery store, your neighbor, or even a complete stranger. Pay attention to your own reaction as you extend yourself. Don't worry about the other person; just make an appropriate contact. Simply get outside yourself in a friendly manner. Make a connection, if only for a few seconds.

Getting outside yourself connects you to others. Stretching to close the gap between yourself and another can repair a relationship and forge a friendship. In contrast, consistently focusing on yourself sends the message to others that you aren't interested, that you don't care or even notice. People who walk around in their own world send a signal that says, "Keep away." Others interpret silence negatively, even if that is not the intention of the silent person. If you withhold eye contact or a polite greeting, most people will take that to mean that you are not interested.

In addition, those who constantly talk about themselves or continually bring the focus back to them give the impression that they are more in search of an audience than a connection. Even if the person is quite charming and can engage people easily, over time the one-way relationship will be unfulfilling for both people involved. If the contact, conversation, or energy goes only one way, it leaves both people alone as well as lonely. Reach out and touch, offer support, be available for others, give what is difficult yet right, and love others to love yourself.

From Noticing to Compassion

Compassion, according to the Dalai Lama, is simply the desire to ease suffering. Millions of Americans watched in horror as the events of 9/11 unfolded. Those of us outside the targeted areas sat for one day, two days, or more, glued to the TV in shock. Those residing in and around New York, Washington, and Shanksville, Pennsylvania, were living with the disaster firsthand in their neighborhoods. Those of us with friends, colleagues, and loved ones in harm's way struggled through jammed phone lines and transportation shutdowns to reach one another for comfort and assistance.

A monumental outreach of aid, supplies, and support came from all over the world. Even the smallest countries did what they could; many of them were happy to repay the kindness they had received in the past when the United States was first on the scene of an international disaster. The tragedy of 9/11 inspired immeasurable acts of compassion. The suffering was so evident, widespread, and powerful, and the desire to ease that suffering was equally powerful.

Compassion has been the key to the ongoing process of healing from the 9/11 attack. In times of deepest sorrow and suffering, human contact and comfort helps the most. Who can forget the story of the firefighters who sacrificed their lives to save others and who were later found dead in the rubble with their arms wrapped around each other? This final act of comfort is an indelible memory of compassion, reminding us how very precious human connection is.

In his latest book, *Toward a True Kinship of Faith,* His Holiness reminds us that compassion is the concept that unites all the world religions. In a lecture to an audience in the United States, His Holiness stated, "I'm not so concerned if you believe in reincarnation. I'm not so concerned if you believe in karma. What concerns me most is that you are compassionate; because if you have compassion you'll have good karma and a good reincarnation!" Then he laughed in his own unique way that just makes others smile and laugh, too.

Knowing yourself and being connected are prerequisites for compassion, so the essential question is "Am I connected?" If so, to whom? What is the nature of your connection? Is it mostly designed for your convenience? Is it a one-way street leading to you? Or are you so desperate for connection that you will become whatever the other person wants you to be, just to be in contact?

Connection implies that there are two separate people coming together to make contact. If you require the other person to be just like you, take part in activities that only you like, and share the opinions that you hold, then ultimately there is only one self in the relationship, and it will be lonely for both people. With only one set of opinions and one set of ideas, the possibilities are limited. The phenomenon also works the other way: if you become like the other person just to please her or gain his favor, then ultimately you'll both be lonely; you'll be without a self, and your friend will be without a companion.

It should go without saying, but we'll say it just to be clear: relationships based on fear or shame also lead to loneliness. If you have given up part of yourself in a relationship because of a fear of retaliation, loss, or punishment, the dishonesty creates a special kind of loneliness. Abandoning your core values to appease another ultimately leaves you both lonely. If you are controlling someone's behavior by these same means—that is, threatening to leave or using your anger—loneliness awaits you also. The connection that prevents loneliness is born of two individuals acting in ways that support their core values as well as the roles of the relationship.

Roles

Intimate connection requires authenticity—that is, being true to your core values—but it also requires the people involved to be true to the appropriate roles, rules, and expectations of the relationship. Roles create order and stability. At work, when each person fulfills the role that he or she was hired to fulfill, it makes for an orderly way of doing business. If an assistant begins to act like the boss, it creates confusion and even chaos. If two employees have equal status according to the organizational chart, yet one bosses the other or treats the other like a subordinate, this causes discord and dissonance. It's not what we'd call a healthy work culture. Role confusion, or what some refer to as boundary violations, are a common source of disconnection in relationships.

You can easily see the importance of roles in families. Take the Jones family as an example: there are the parents and two children, ages thirteen and sixteen. Thus, in this family there are three separate units, each with different role expectations: (1) the spousal unit, (2) the parental unit, and (3) the sibling unit.

The role of the spousal unit is to enable the adults to get their adult needs met with each other; this unit has privacy from the children. The role of partner, husband, or wife usually includes being a best friend, confidant, financial partner, social partner, and sexual and sensual partner. Having a committed partner commonly means that there is someone on your side, someone in your corner, someone to whom you are a priority, and someone to whom you have pledged fidelity, support, and care. When you are in a committed love relationship, there is the expectation that a certain level of your energy and interest belongs to your partner and no one else.

Obviously there are wide variations on this theme. Happiness in relationships occurs most frequently when what you expect is what you get. Couples have all kinds of contracts about the roles they play. You probably know couples who say they are happy, but you wonder, "How on earth does that work?" It probably works because the roles they have agreed on are being met.

Parenting is different from partnering. Partnering is about adults getting their adult needs met, whereas parenting is about the adults providing love and structure for the children. Parenting is also different from being a friend. Friendship is a relationship of peers—two people with the same power and responsibility. Parenting is not about being best friends with your kids; it's about providing love and structure. The adults get to be the grown-ups; that's the good news and the bad news.

When children are permitted to act like adults before their time by bossing other family members and demanding the privileges of adults without the responsibilities, this invites chaos and ruins the connection. Kids will fight for power and control, but when they get it, it creates anxiety and resentment from all other units in the family—including them. Kids will ultimately resent and disrespect parents who let them rule the family. The sense of entitlement that develops when kids are allowed to rule the family sets them up for unrealistic expectations and disappointment later in life. Entitled children become entitled adults. Entitlement prevents intimate connection and ultimately breeds loneliness.

Siblings have important roles in the family because being a sibling is how one learns social skills and give-and-take. Brothers and sisters can temper a child's sense of entitlement quite naturally; in this way, siblings teach one another how to get along with others. An only child will need access to friends and extended family members to learn these skills and establish appropriate boundaries.

The family provides the first opportunity for most of us to learn the importance of roles, rules, and regulations. Roles provide protective boundaries between you and another person. Honoring roles and boundaries makes for a clear connection, because they create safety as well as respect for each person involved. If you grew up in a family in which the roles were unclear—for example, the parents didn't provide love and structure, or you were not protected from harsh words or abuse, or you were allowed to run rampant over other family members —then you have undoubtedly struggled in some of your relationships as an adult. Take heart, however; the principles of this book apply to you just as much as to those who were fortunate enough to have been protected by clear roles and responsible parenting. Knowing who you are is a lifelong process; so is knowing and understanding the roles you play in others' lives.

Differentiation

In Chapter 3 we focused on the question "Who Am I?" because knowing yourself and being clear about your values and guiding principles enables you to be a separate and vital person when connecting to another. Without this differentiation, there is nothing with which to connect. A relationship will have little or no energy without two viable people involved. When you know who you are, you can be objective about your own thoughts and feelings and, just as important, separate your thoughts and feelings from those of others. You can differentiate yourself from another person. This way there is a self that is available for connection. Two separate beings make for a far more interesting and viable relationship.

Differentiation is a term used in systems theory that describes an evolutionary advantage derived from being in a relationship with people who have a multitude of abilities. As life becomes more complex, it is to humans' benefit to have access to a variety of skills and resources, because no one person can know everything or be capable of performing all tasks. When aptitudes differ among individuals, the resource bank becomes broader and creates a survival advantage. Intelligent, well-adjusted people can see the advantage of embracing difference. They are stimulated by and even attracted to people who bring different skills and talents to the relationship.

An environment that is constantly changing requires a great deal of skill adaptation and flexibility in order to acclimate. Anyone living in this day and age knows how quickly the world around us is changing. Just trying to keep up with the most basic technology is like a full-time job for most of us. Adapting to change is a part of life in the twenty-first century, because changes are occurring at warp speed. More than ever, we need to be free to develop our individual talents and to support others in doing the same. When you know who you are and support others in knowing who they are, everyone benefits.

Differentiation is based on knowing who you are and understanding that the roles you play are necessary for true connection. If you try to make a connection by adapting your behavior to please someone else, such as by abandoning who you really are or by abandoning your core values to become more like that person, the relationship will ultimately end in loneliness. If a relationship requires that the two of you be alike, how are you going to maintain stability when circumstances change? Honoring and celebrating difference makes a relationship flourish.

Here are four simple steps for acknowledging differentiation and creating connection:

1. Show up.
2. Pay attention.
3. Comprehend.
4. Act congruently.

Showing up means practicing mindful presence. You know who you are, and you act in a way that is congruent with your guiding principles. You arrive with authenticity. You are acting like yourself, not someone else. We have spent so much of this book helping you to determine who you are so that you will recognize yourself when you show up. Showing up also means that you have to make time and energy available for connection. It means arriving and attending, getting your body and your soul to the agreed-upon place on time.

Paying attention means tuning in to the other person. This is why differentiation is so important; it allows you to separate your thoughts and feelings from another's. You know where you stop and the other person begins. Paying attention enables you to be available for him or her and not just be standing in your own world. Tuning in means using all your senses—seeing with your eyes, hearing with your ears, and so on—to take in information. Just having your body present doesn't mean that you are paying attention. How many times have you been with someone who is more tuned in to his or her own thoughts or surroundings—even a cell phone—than you? It doesn't make for a meaningful connection.

Comprehending means paying attention long enough and mindfully enough to understand the other person. Again, this requires separating your own ideas, thoughts, and feelings from those of others. We're not implying that this is easy; it takes practice. Comprehending also means that you tune in long enough to see the other person's point of view and get a feeling for what he or she is feeling. You might even start to empathize, to feel what he or she is feeling.

Acting congruently means behaving in a way that shows you've been paying attention. When Daniel comforted Ngawang, he showed that he'd been paying attention. That he was still sitting with her well over an hour after he noticed her sorrow showed that he understood and cared about the depth of her grief. Daniel had a strong desire to aid in easing her suffering, and his actions were congruent with this desire.

The four requirements are extremely vital to connection, so let's explore them further.

Showing Up

We spent a whole chapter on "Who Am I?" because knowing who you are is a prerequisite for making an authentic connection to another person. If you don't know who you are, the signal you send to others can't be clear or dependable. Knowing who you are and then being that person in a mindful, conscious manner enables you to show up consistently and in a meaningful way. This mindful presence has an interesting effect on others.

You can experience this presence with infants when you engage with them. They are so attentive—taking in every nuance, every signal from your face, your body, your tone of voice. This mindful presence is part of their charm. They really see you and respond acutely when they hear your voice or feel your touch. An infant who is only hours-old can recognize the scent of the mother and discern it from a stranger's. Babies demonstrate mindful presence as if their lives depended upon it— because they do.

Showing up in a way that is both mindful and present has a powerful effect when exhibited by adults also. As we mentioned earlier, there were eight of us who traveled to Dharamsala to participate in the private audience with His Holiness the Dalai Lama. It was at the generosity of Jhampa, who was granted the audience, that we were honored with this privilege. Among the eight of us were four practicing Buddhists and four academic types. One of the Buddhists was Jésus, a delightful man from Mexico who spoke English as well as Spanish. After the formal visit with His Holiness, as we were processing the experience, Jésus made an observation that held many important lessons. He said, "When we first sat down in the room with His Holiness, I thought, *Well, this isn't so unusual or magical,* but then I looked around the room . . ."—Jésus lowered his voice, opened his eyes wide, and whispered in reverence—". . . and everyone was radiant."

The Dalai Lama is so mindfully present, whether it's in a private audience or an audience of thousands. We've heard him in many settings, and he has the same effect each time. He shows up in a very real fashion. There's no pretense, just presence—and that presence is extremely engaging. It is such an honor to have someone show up in such a present state. He wasn't multitasking, and he wasn't rushing us; he was present and patient, and the experience was powerful. There's nothing like someone being truly present to get your attention. It gives you goose bumps and makes the blood rush to your head because your brain is firing on all its cylinders. When someone truly shows up and is available, it engages you immediately. You don't have to be the Dalai Lama to have a powerful effect on others; showing up with presence will be powerful enough.

How Well Do You Show Up?

People, young and old alike, evaluate relationships around holidays, birthdays, and other special occasions. How dependable are you for showing up at these times? What about funerals, graduations, weddings, and anniversaries? Do you show up only when it's convenient or guaranteed to be fun for you? Do you show up when it might mean more to others than it does to you? Do you show up even when you have to go alone and might not know a lot of people? A relationship can be forged or forgotten by the choices you make about when and where you show up.

When you do show up, are you truly present? It's not enough to have your body there; your soul has to come along. Do you show up with presence and a sense of curiosity about others? Are you a willing participant in the planned event? Can you be counted on to follow protocol, use your manners, and extend a helping hand? Your presence is powerful; connection requires that you spend it wisely.

"I contend that I have the best friends in the world," Pat declares. "I say this because they have rescued me over and over throughout my life. When I was in grade school, I literally had a bed of my own at more than one friend's house. When life got too tough in my home, I'd just go stay at Bonnie's or Barbara's, where I was always welcome. (I lived in a small town where everyone knew your private circumstances; it was clear that I needed a port in a storm.) As I got older, I hung on to some of these friends even though I moved across the country and never again lived in my hometown. I travel back to West Virginia not because I have any family members there, but because I have friends there.

"When I arrived in Austin, and didn't know anyone," she continues, "the first thing I did was to look for friends. I made it a tangible goal. I put time, money, and effort into making new friends and forging connections. I made one new friend through a professional group, and I met a couple more at church. Through these connections my social circle began to expand. Nancy introduced me to Luci, then Brigida, who introduced me to Stephanie. Noelie introduced me to Cindie and Sheila, who introduced me to JoAnn. You get the picture. A loosely knitted group started to form from one friend and another.

"Then," Pat recalls, "my friend Kappie's husband died, and the funeral was scheduled to be held hours away in east Texas. This one event coalesced the girlfriends. Despite the distance and the difficulty in getting there (it takes two flights or one long drive), the group managed to arrive en masse, attend the funeral, and organize a dinner for those in attendance. Showing up for this occasion changed the loose-knit group into the Girlfriends, with a capital *G*.

"Since that time twenty-five years ago," she concludes, "this coalition has supported each individual as we married, divorced, buried, birthed, graduated, celebrated, and lived through chemotherapy, bypass surgery, infidelity, boom and bust, liposuction and Botox, detox, treatment, and terrorist attacks. We've been to Paris, Texas, and Paris, France, as well as Australia, Sweden, Norway, Switzerland, Mexico, Honduras, and Senegal. This group has supported me in every way: physically, financially, and emotionally—you name it, and all with love and grace. The Girlfriends really show up!"

Friendship is a powerful force; it is one of the deepest forms of connection. You don't get to pick your biological or adoptive family as a child, but you do get to pick your intentional family as an adult. Friendships are forged through the firestorms of life. You've heard of fair-weather friends—the ones who show up only when it's fun or convenient for them. Good friends show up in all weather, whether it's convenient for them or not. Showing up just might be the better part of friendship—or of any meaningful connection.

By now you are probably getting the picture that it's not enough to simply know your core values and understand the kind of person you want to be. You also have to practice being that person—when you're alone, when you're with others, under stress and even duress. Relationships can bring out the best or the worst in us. It's often more of a challenge to be true to yourself and follow your core values when you are engaging with the people you love or care for the most. This is why the practice of mindful meditation is important. The habits have to be ingrained so that when you show up, you will be authentic and differentiated—that is, your true self. If you think about the people whom you trust most, you will undoubtedly realize that they are the people who show up for you consistently and congruently.

Paying Attention

Imagine the following conversation. Jake and Sara meet for lunch. Jake says, "I walked around the lake this morning, and it was so hot I think I was on the verge of heat exhaustion." Sara replies, "My neighbor had the same experience yesterday when he was cleaning out the garage because this is the weekend for the bulk pickup in our neighborhood and his wife is expecting their second child and she's trying to get the house ready for the new baby that I gave the baby shower for last week even though I am getting ready for the bar exam, which I can't believe is only three weeks away."

You get the impression that Sara was paying more attention to the movie in her own head than to Jake, her lunch companion. As she talked, her subjects moved further and further from the information in Jake's initial disclosure; she seemed to be entertaining herself instead of paying attention to her friend or maintaining a connecting conversation. Jake might stay engaged for a short while in such a one-way conversation, but if it went on for very long, her mind would likely wander—and wonder. The connection wouldn't be very satisfying for either of them, because Sara wasn't really paying attention. She was also far from the concept of right speech, which we learned from the Dalai Lama.

Right Speech and Paying Attention

If you are paying attention to someone, it will be evident in your speech. Right speech, or mindful talking, requires that you pay attention and stay focused. Before our visit with His Holiness, we were well aware of his views on right speech. We didn't want to embarrass ourselves or waste his time in idle chatter or inane questions. Even if we hadn't known this about him from his teachings, the protocol leading up to the visit would have given us a hint, because you don't just walk in and have a chat with the Dalai Lama. The process we went through before we met with His Holiness took about four hours.

We were staying in McLeod Ganj, which is about one and a quarter miles from the Central Tibetan Administration (CTA), where the Dalai Lama lives and houses his administration that runs schools, health services, cultural activities, and economic development projects for the Tibetan community in exile. We were going to walk from McLeod Ganj to the compound in Dharamsala. Our appointment was for 11:00 AM, so we set out at about 7:00 AM. Along the way we followed a path that was partly paved and partly dirt; it was well-worn by monks and villagers who use it for making their daily prayers and practicing moving meditation. It's amazing and somewhat beyond words to be surrounded by people who are all going about life in such a reverent fashion. That walk, which most of us took every morning for two weeks, was enough to make a shift in our souls. It didn't matter that we were among people who spoke a different language or even prayed in a different fashion; the power of the connection was there.

The second part of the journey that day was past the Namoval Monastery, which was founded shortly after the Dalai Lama took up residence in Dharamsala. We were curious to see the complex up close, because from our hotel across the valley and up the mountain we could see and hear all kinds of activities going on at the monastery pretty much around the clock. We heard calls to prayer, music and drumming, lots of laughter, and even the raucous sounds of debate. The presence of the monks in their maroon robes adds so much to the experience in and around McLeod Ganj and Dharamsala. They are everywhere, just going about life.

Once we were past the monastery and had approached the grounds of the CTA, we had to go through the first round of security. It's no secret that His Holiness, because of his stance on Tibet, has enemies around the world. One of the reasons Dharamsala was chosen as a site for the headquarters is that there's only one road in and one road out, making access visible and easier to protect. On the grounds is a beautiful temple, which Jhampa toured with us, recalling his years of study and practice during his twelve-year residence. Whether or not you are a practicing Buddhist, it's inspiring to be in a location that holds such special meaning for others. Jhampa wisely scheduled time in the temple for us to prepare ourselves for the visit to follow.

To enter the actual grounds on which the Dalai Lama resides, you must go through yet another round of security. This time it was more like airport security plus a registration process. At this point we knew we were getting closer, because there was a solemnity and a lack of activity as the two people who greeted us invited us to sit for just a few more minutes. The quiet was offset somewhat by our inner excitement and anxiety. We knew that we were going to ask His Holiness for permission to use his teachings in a book designed to help people in the Western world, but we didn't know how that conversation would go or what he might ask of us.

Just the idea of speaking to someone of his stature was both exciting and intimidating, to say the least. Everything we knew about him implied that we would be respected and received politely, but what if we wasted his time? What if we said something stupid? We knew his teachings about idle chatter and right speech; what if we fell into the first category and not the second? The period in that quiet waiting area seemed to go on for a long time—we were so near and yet so far.

Finally, someone appeared from within the compound and ushered us into yet another waiting room. This time it was more like a living room or a sitting area. On three of the four walls were glass shelves that held trophies, medals, decorations, acknowledgments, and the grand award: the Nobel Peace Prize. You had to look at everything to find the Nobel Prize award, because it was simply displayed as one of many items and held no more prominent place than that held by other awards from around the world. There were proclamations from presidents and heads of state, plaques for service to humanity, numerous honorary doctoral degrees, a gold medal—from the National Autonomous University of Mexico, not the Olympics—and peace prize acknowledgments galore.

The entire room was a humanistic hall of fame. There wasn't time to take in every item because we were distracted by a commotion outside the room that indicated that something was happening. Someone opened the doors and hurried us out onto the porch, where we saw a group of monks bowing low and backing out of a room (for practicing Buddhists, the honorary custom is for your head to be no higher than His Holiness's head). We wondered if we should do that, too, but were reminded of Jhampa's words: "His Holiness expects Westerners to act like Westerners."

Passing the bowing monks, we entered His Holiness's living room. There he was, waiting to receive us. Whoa! That was a moment. But there was no time to sit and take it all in; with no time wasted, it was time to speak. There was no impatience; just readiness, so Jhampa made a few comments and then turned the time over to us. Gulp. The first few words were surreal, like "Is this really my voice talking?" But somehow the words came out about how our hearts were heavy with the burdens of those who are lonely and long for connection, and we respectfully request permission to use His Holiness's writings and teachings to address this issue.

With little or no hesitation, His Holiness looked briefly at his secretary, then shrugged his shoulders and said, "Sure, why not?" And that was it. All the rehearsing, planning, waiting, and anticipating came to an end with "Sure, why not?" Right speech; no idle words; mission accomplished—but nobody moved. His Holiness looked around the room, inviting more conversation—but more on that later.

Looking back on this day, we now realize how each step before we met with His Holiness was important. The time and effort we invested certainly made the point that this wasn't a casual occasion or a drop-in visit. Jhampa had been waiting for years. He had to apply well in advance for the audience to be granted. Needless to say, his kindness and his willingness to include us created a turning point in our lives. It also gave us a powerful experience of preparing for right speech; we had made far too much effort to waste the time with idle chatter. We took time to pay attention to the experience before us.

From the Dalai Lama, we learned that right speech means the following:

1. Avoid lies, deceit, slander, and harsh words.
2. Avoid idle chatter.
3. Speak the truth.
4. Speak in a friendly, warm, and gentle fashion.

Practicing right speech can improve communication and thus connection. It's pretty evident that lies, deceit, slander, and harsh words prevent connection. People sometimes create their own loneliness by acting in this way. What isn't so easy to see is how idle chatter can be just as destructive to relationships. Go back to the conversation between Sara and Jake. How long could you stay engaged with Sara if she persisted in talking in such an idle fashion? It may be entertaining to her, but it certainly doesn't inspire connection. It makes you wonder to whom she's really talking. Is she paying attention at all? What she's doing is more like verbal self-stimulation than an attempt at connection.

This example of conversation may seem unreal to you, exaggerated to an extreme, but we assure you it is not. As you become more mindful of your actions and clearer about your core values and who you are, you'll begin to pay closer attention and notice when you or others use idle chatter to fill precious time that could be used for more meaningful connection.

What constitutes meaningful connection in talking? It's pretty clear what lies, deceit, slander, and harsh words are, but what is idle chatter? To answer that question, we've created a table of information that invites connection. We call it the levels of connection. It certainly hasn't been tested for more than 2,500 years, as Buddhist practices have, but we hope that it will help you to be more mindful of your verbal communication and to understand the spirit of the difference between idle chatter and meaningful exchange.

The Levels of Connection

Level 1 Physical presence. Showing up. Basic talking and listening. Can include small talk, polite exchange, maintenance information. If this type of conversation goes on for too long, it becomes idle chatter.

"I can't believe this humidity."
"How are you?" "Fine, and you?"
"Did you get milk?" "Yes."

Level 2 The subject is of general interest to at least one person. If this conversation continues, it becomes one-sided and self-absorbed. Move on to Level 3 to avoid idle chatter.

"I like this restaurant because you can eat outside."
"I found the perfect dress for your sister's wedding."
"The Longhorns won in baseball in extra innings!"

Level 3 The subject is of general interest to both people. The conversation begins to move away from idle chatter to an engaging exchange. Both people connect to the conversation and its content.

"How do you like your phone?"
"Our neighbor's house was robbed last night."
"So what did you like about the movie?"
"There was a big fire in the building next to your work."
"The Badgers won in baseball in extra innings."
"I found out why our electric bill was so high last month."
"I like to spend time with you because you have such a good attitude about life."

Level 4 The subject is of immediate interest to at least one person. The conversation is more engaging, and the two people are moving toward connection.

"I'll cook dinner tonight; do you want fish or vegetable stir-fry?"
"What shall we do this weekend?"
"Would you show me how to program this so I don't have to keep asking you to do it?"
"I'm really upset about my job. Would you help me by just listening for a few minutes?"

The Levels of Connection (continued)

Level 5 The subject is of immediate interest to both people. The conversation is engaging; it shows you've been paying attention.

"How can I help?"
"Something hilarious happened today . . ."
"Remember the time . . ."
"You were right about . . ."
"I found a way to save money on utilities."
"I had a nice thought about you today . . ."

Level 6 The subject is of mutual interest, but one person is taking ownership of a behavior or a feeling. The immediacy of the subject—talking about *now*—adds to the engagement.

"I'm sorry about last night . . ."
"I like spending time with you."
"I messed up at work . . ."
"I can't always express what I mean."
"I'm interested, but right now I have to get this done."
"Something that's really important to me is . . ."

Level 7 The conversation includes immediacy (something that is currently happening), ownership, and inclusion of the other person. Including the other person is engaging.

"Tonight I'd like us to . . ."
"Something I'd like us to do together is . . ."
"I'd like to spend some time with you."
"You look great."
"I always enjoy my time with you."
"Did you hear about Claudia's doctor's visit?"

Level 8 The conversation includes immediacy, ownership, inclusion, and emotion. Emotional expression invites attention and participation.

"I love you."
"I miss you."
"Your friendship means so much to me."
"I admire the way you do that."
"You make me a better person."
"You are fun to hang out with."

The Levels of Connection (continued)

Level 9	Vulnerability is expressed about something other than the relationship. Vulnerability invites compassion and deep connection.	"Mom's not doing well." "I'm worried about my job." "I'm not sure I'm strong enough to say no." "The tests came back positive." "I'm having trouble coping." "I'm so sad." "I feel so useless; I wish I could help."
Level 10	Vulnerability is expressed about the relationship. Vulnerability is risky, but it can build deep trust and connection.	*"You mean so much to me."* *"I miss our time together."* *"Your love makes me a better person."* *"I don't feel as close to you."* *"I'm sorry I was late; I know how that upsets you."* *"I'm going to have to cancel our plans."* *"I don't know where we are going to get the money."* *"Our sex life is a serious issue."*

We use these categories mainly to make a point: what you say and how you say it does make an impression, and it either invites connection or doesn't invite connection. Only about 10 percent of what we communicate is through our words—the rest is by our tone, body posture, and facial expressions—but words do count. As you read through the levels, we hope that you can get a sense of how they differ in inviting closeness. As you pay attention to the way in which you show up and connect in a relationship, we invite you to ponder the following: Are your words congruent with (1) who you are, (2) the message you want to send about connection, and (3) the nature of the relationship?

The designated levels of connection are important for close relationships, but they also have an important function when you're meeting new people or dealing with acquaintances and coworkers. As you read the levels, you can see that there is a growing sense of familiarity; this is purposeful. It would be incongruent to use the more intimate levels with a person you have just met or with a person at work with whom you have only a work relationship. It would be incongruent with polite exchange and rewarding connection and also constitute a boundary violation.

Before you take a conversation into vulnerable areas, make sure that this is appropriate and congruent with the nature of the relationship. Baring your soul to someone who is showing no signs of interest or availability will be disappointing to you, to say the least. Treating a work relationship like a friendship can also lead to disappointment and cause problems. The temptation to cross the line at work is great because of the long hours we spend together, but doing so can have serious consequences over time. (That's a whole other book!) It is best not to cross that line to begin with. Pay attention to whom and how you pay attention.

Comprehending

Once you show up and pay attention, comprehending becomes vital to intimate connection. To comprehend means to understand or grasp. It comes from the Latin *comprehendere*, "to come together." When someone understands you, grasps who you are, and comprehends your uniqueness, and you are tuned in enough to notice that this is happening, connection occurs.

Similarly, when you have been paying attention and truly understand another person, and he or she knows that you understand, this creates a moment of connection. This mutual knowing creates a gratifying form of communication known as limbic resonance. The resonance is caused by an echo of remembering the other times that this person (or someone else) has seen you, understood you, or provided life-giving attention.

Because of our early dependency, the human brain is biased toward activities such as deep connection. A baby survives because someone shows up, pays attention long enough to understand the baby's needs, and then acts appropriately. This process is directly connected to the baby's survival. An infant cannot survive alone. Someone has to comprehend the baby's needs and act accordingly. Thus, when someone comprehends you, even as an adult, there is a memory, a good feeling, and a sense of anticipation that your needs are being met.

Because connection is vital to life, the human brain continues to value it and depend on it. Once you mature, you can survive alone, but you won't thrive alone. We are designed to be in relationship because our odds of survival are greatly increased with the aid and support of at least a few other people. When you connect to someone, especially someone who comprehends who you are, it creates a bit of magic as it imprints your psyche. These magic moments are simply markers to remind you that you are safe; you are not alone.

Acting Congruently

If you show up in a way that is congruent with your values, pay attention long enough to understand where the other person is coming from, and then act in a way that is congruent with your knowledge of this person, you have done your part to make connection happen. If the other person does the same thing in return, connection will happen and loneliness will dissipate.

Congruence has two major components: harmony with yourself and harmony with the other person. Guess which one is more difficult.

After our experience in India, personal congruence became more difficult. If you have ever taken three weeks off for a relaxing vacation, you know how hard the reentry process is. The day or two before you return home, you sometimes feel anxiety from knowing what awaits you. We had that type of experience, but multiplied. While we were in India, we had the luxury of being totally focused on showing up, paying attention, comprehending, and acting congruently. With Jhampa leading us, making sure that we got food and shelter, not to mention entertainment and spiritual guidance, it was easy.

When we came home, it was another story! There were the usual everyday tasks that awaited, three weeks' worth of work that had not been tended to, and, of course, friends and loved ones to catch up with. This wasn't the challenge, however. The challenge was how to integrate the renewed core values we had been practicing in India into our daily lives back home. We'll spare you the details of how difficult this was; the bottom-line advice from us is this: just focus on the next right thing. Decide on your core values, keep them in the forefront of your mind at every moment of every day, and then do the right thing. The Dalai Lama calls this creating right action, and it consists of the following steps:

1. Abstain from harming any living things.
2. Avoid sexual misconduct; keep sexual relationships harmless to others.
3. Develop emotional regulation.
4. Practice self-control and self-discipline.

When you abstain from harming any living things, you gain a deeper connection with the world around you. Of course, living things include the people you encounter in everyday life. Regardless of how you are treated, do no harm; don't let someone else decide your core values.

When His Holiness discusses right action, he includes all sentient beings—that is, any organism that is able to see or feel. You'll have to decide for yourself how to implement this step of right action. We can guarantee one outcome: the more respectful you are toward other living beings, the less lonely you will be.

Sexual misconduct covers a broad range of activities. In this day and age, when even texting has become sexting and you cannot avoid sexually stimulating images if you use technology even in the least, conducting yourself appropriately in the realm of sex becomes more challenging. Sex is such a powerful force because it is a drive, like hunger; it is necessary for the survival of the species. It also feels good and provides a surge of pleasure; therefore, it's tempting to use it just for fun, regardless of the consequences. Sex is also a bonding activity. The oxytocin rush that triggers orgasm also bonds two people and even creates a period of amnesia right after sex during which you forget any harshness or mistreatment that has occurred between the two of you. Sex can be complicated, but it can be managed successfully if you keep your core values in mind.

Emotional regulation is the big one. Strong negative emotions destroy relationships, break connection, and foster loneliness. It's difficult to maintain a close, connected relationship with someone whose emotions erupt like a land mine. The word *emotion* comes from the root "to move." Emotions tell us what to do. The problem is that emotions come from past experiences and often lead us astray. If you are in the habit of getting angry or have been taught to "get your anger out" then expressing anger feels natural. The problem is that this makes you feel better but it makes others feel worse. It drives people away.

Your emotional brain is biased toward the negative—that is, it immediately looks at the worst-case scenario. To your emotional brain, it's better to be safe than sorry. The reason for this is simple: in terms of your safety, it's better to think that a stick is a snake than to think that a snake is a stick. Emotions, if you follow them without mindfulness, can make you overreact and drive other people away. This is why mindful meditation teaches you to simply watch your emotions and not run with them or follow them.

If you learned years ago to "follow your feelings," that was bad advice. If you follow your feelings, you are essentially re-creating your worst past moments. That is a one-way street to loneliness. You must learn to be mindful of your emotions and then follow your core values, regardless of how it feels. Do the right thing, and the emotions will eventually follow.

Self-control and self-discipline will draw the right people to you.

Letting go and being out of control might be entertaining for a short time, but this isn't a lifestyle you want to pursue if you long for connection. How can anyone depend on you when you are unpredictable or have a proclivity for acting out? You might have short-term friends, but they will tire of the drama and ultimately seek companionship with people who have more self-discipline. Self-control doesn't have to mean stodgy or boring. Look at your core values. This person doesn't have to be a dullard; if you practice right action by acting congruently with your core values, you will be sought after as a friend and a confidant and never be lonely again.

Making an Imprint

People come into your life for a reason, for a season, for a lesson, or for a lifetime. If someone has noticed you, even for a moment, the print of contact still remains. What type of print are *you* leaving? Do you make the most of opportunities to notice wherever you go? Have you taken the opportunity to get outside your own frame of reference and enter the world of another person, even for a moment? Here are some ideas and queries to invite you into someone else's world:

1. What if you changed your mind about someone? This person might have disappointed you or hurt you, ignored you or betrayed you. If you changed your mind, what would that look like and feel like?
2. What kind of friend are you? How would someone who knows you describe your friendship? What would you need to do to be a better friend?
3. What role do you play in your family? How do you contribute to family cohesion and compassion?
4. How willing are you to inconvenience yourself for the sake of friendship or connection?
5. How do you invest in the relationships that you have?

Jon's Practice of Loving-Kindness

For the past decade, I have made yearly trips to the Buddhist nation of Thailand, where *metta*, a Pali word that means "loving-kindness," is part of daily life. Metta basically means to practice loving-kindness with others. It involves a nonclinging form of love in which you wish that all people be well. This creates a positive mind-set toward people you love, people you hardly know, and people you find downright irritating. The level of giving and thinking of others that I experience in Thailand is difficult to describe. I tell my friends it's like the attention that Elvis or Michael Jackson must have felt from their fans.

If I take a bite of cake, within minutes four more pieces appear. If I look at something and ask what is that, I will find several in my room later in the day. The thoughtfulness is carried out with deep caring and no thought of getting something in return. When I lecture, I need to allow equal time for photos, the receiving of gifts, and a summary in both Thai and English from many audience members with deep thanks for my gift of knowledge.

At first I felt special and revered; however, I finally asked my friend Tipa what this was all about. After all, I need extra luggage for each return trip just to take all of the offerings of food, trinkets, cloth, apparel, and figurines I'm given each time I visit. Tipa said that this was metta, something that all Thai people strive to do.

It was through many months of daily metta practice that I learned to truly connect with others. I changed my view and my understanding of people, and I worked hard at validating everyone I met. As I thought differently, I began acting differently, and random acts of kindness became more frequent. I reached out to colleagues and friends and worked at being generous for the right reasons. I did things for others rather than to build up my self-worth. My therapy practice shifted significantly as I focused on strengths and assets and actively validated clients' rights and decisions.

Dramatic changes occurred as I became more present, honest, and genuinely empathic to others. Diagnosis, labels, and judgments were disappearing as my internal presence became visible. I began taking risks and helped others by challenging the ways they handled life difficulties. I encouraged them to look at life in a different, more meaningful way. As my connections to others became more real and compassionate, this carried over to all living things. Ants, bugs, spiders, flies, and even mosquitoes were spared, because they were no longer my enemies. Learning to live in harmony changed the way I danced through life. As I changed, my outlook changed and I could not help but notice that people as well as critters were treating me better.

Exercise 15: **Metta Meditation**

By the graciousness of the Thai people, we offer you a gift: the practice of metta. This positive practice makes it possible for you to have some control over whether a connection takes place. Having a positive, open, accepting, and caring attitude will serve as a magnet in attracting others.

To create self-control and to better understand your role in relationships, we urge a daily practice of *metta* meditation. This is a process in which you begin with deep breaths and focus on yourself.

As you sit comfortably and begin to focus on your breath, we invite you to create a clear picture of yourself. It's as though you are sitting across from yourself, watching as you relax and breathe. Once you have a clear picture, lay this blessing on the self in front of you: "I wish that you be peaceful, happy, safe, and free." See yourself accept the blessing. Pay attention to how you feel as you accept the blessing.

Now move your gaze to picture someone close to you sitting in front of you, and say to this person, "I wish that you be peaceful, happy, safe, and free." Notice the reaction as the blessing is received.

Now, in your mind's eye, move on to people whom you see but seldom notice, such as those who serve your food, those who ride with you on elevators, and those with whom you interact each day. Picture each person and wish that he or she be peaceful, happy, safe, and free.

Finally, picture someone with whom you have a conflict or a disagreement or whom you simply do not like. Picture this person and say, "I wish that you be peaceful, happy, safe, and free."

Metta practice, showering others with your blessings, can forge connections you may not have thought possible. Showing up, paying attention, comprehending others, and acting congruently will create a life in which you will never be lonely again.

5

Am I Living in Community?

I AM OF THE OPINION THAT MY LIFE BELONGS TO THE WHOLE COMMUNITY AND AS LONG AS I LIVE, IT IS MY PRIVILEGE TO DO FOR IT WHATEVER I CAN. I WANT TO BE THOROUGHLY USED UP WHEN I DIE, FOR THE HARDER I WORK THE MORE I LIVE.

—George Bernard Shaw, author

Earlier in the book we mentioned that one of the easiest ways to prevent loneliness is to do something every day that represents your core values and leads to connection. For example, being helpful to a friend reminds you who you are and at the same time strengthens your intimate connection to another person. Practicing your core values in this way ultimately builds a bridge of contact, and you begin to feel personally congruent as well as secure in your intimate relationships.

The reach of loneliness goes beyond your intimate circle, however; it extends outward into the community to which you belong, and only by investing in this community can you ward off the loneliness that occurs when you don't have a sense of belonging. Close friends and family make you feel secure, but belonging comes from community. Investing time and energy in making contact where you live—whether it be through your neighborhood, a civic organization, a religious affiliation, or social activities—makes you feel part of the community. You won't feel lonely when you are involved in activities that benefit a larger group of people. Investing yourself in a community is one of the most powerful forces in preventing loneliness. Research is so clear about the benefits of community that it just might fall into the category of a quick fix for loneliness.

Communities come in all shapes and sizes. They are formed around religion, race, profession, location, social values, common interests, and hobbies or pastimes—you name it. Thich Nhat Hanh, the well-known Vietnamese monk and author, even travels around the world with two hundred members of his Plum Village community. You are probably a member of several communities, such as the residents of a city, the fans of a sports team, an alumni association, or a religious group. Community alleviates the loneliness that occurs when you don't feel connected to the wider world around you.

Loneliness comes in different forms, and the five not-so-easy pieces (the five questions that are the chapter titles in this section) represent different sources of loneliness. It is important to understand each source to ensure that you will never be lonely again.

The first type, addressed by the question "Who Am I?" is associated with the alienation from self and unclear core values. This loneliness can be offset by knowing who you are and acting out your core values, which helps you to live your life in terms of what is important to you. If loneliness creeps in, all you have to do is ask the following: What would a loving person do about this? What would a fun person do right now? What would a person with a sense of adventure do? Answer these questions with your core values, and you will know the next step away from loneliness. In this manner, knowing who you are prevents loneliness by providing a clear path toward connection—to yourself as well as to others.

The second type of loneliness is addressed by the question "Am I Connected?" and comes from lack of intimate connection. Close contact with a few people can provide you with a sense of security that offsets the isolated feelings of loneliness. You can have purpose and clarity about who you are, but if you are not intimately connected to at least a few people, you are going to feel lonely and less secure, for who is going to come to your aid and share good times and bad? Having ongoing contact with people who support you gives you a sense of security and stability.

In this chapter we introduce a third type of loneliness. It comes from a feeling that you don't belong and can be alleviated only by the experience of living in community, which provides a sense of belonging. Charles Darwin pointed out that animals without an obvious advantage like brute strength, size, or speed survive by belonging to a pack. They live in a group—or a community, so to speak—and the group force becomes the means by which to compete with forces that are stronger than any individual within the group.

Psychologist Alfred Adler described belonging as a basic human need. According to Adler (cited in a book Jon has coauthored entitled *Adlerian Therapy*), "Group life proved to be a necessity because it enabled man, through a division of labor, to solve problems in which the individual would have been condemned to failure." Even though most of us don't need a group to hunt for our food or ward off the threat of large predators, we still experience the longing for belonging, just as we did centuries ago.

Loneliness, as we stated earlier, is a drive—an innate force compelling you toward not only survival but also happiness and success. A large part of both happiness and success comes from the sense of belonging, which in turn comes from a bond with people from the broader community. These are people outside your intimate circle of friends and family. Bonding with a community of people can occur through common interests, but you must participate to feel as though you belong. Simply identifying yourself as a Bears fan, a Republican, or a Presbyterian won't do the job; you have to show up, donate time, and commune with others who share your affiliation. The sense of belonging comes from involvement.

One of the most potent experiences of community occurs when you reach out to people you don't know who simply happen to share space on Earth with you. You can do this by joining an organization, or you can come up with your own unique way. A great example of a unique community in Austin, Texas, is a serendipitous group that gathers for what's known as Monday Night Pizza. Here's how it happened.

Twenty years ago, Judith and Steven were faced with a challenge that many parents face: how to get their grown son, Christian, to visit them more often. Even in those days, when the pace was slower, kids still had lives of their own, places to go, and people to see. So the Frandens became creative: they invited their son to come watch Monday night football, and to sweeten the deal, they offered to provide free pizza and any beverage of choice. That was enough to lure Christian back home once a week, and pretty soon others started to join in. Christian's friends were happy to come by for football and free food; what's not to love about that?

But it wasn't even just the younger set that saw the benefit in a weekly schedule of fun and fellowship; soon Judith and Steven's friends joined in. Then their housemate, Dr. "Mac", and his own cadre of comrades started showing up. Pretty soon Monday Night Pizza became an institution.

Times changed and Christian moved away, so the original rationale no longer applied. Nevertheless, Monday Night Pizza had developed a life of its own. Christian may have left town, but the tradition stayed put. Now, twenty years later, every Monday night you can still go to the house that has a "please walk right in" sign on the door, introduce yourself, and be welcomed.

Monday Night Pizza has several unique aspects. First, the "build it and they will come" edict certainly applies. All that was required to get this tradition started was for someone to have the idea and then follow through; after that, the hosts just let it happen naturally. The weekly social, which began as a family gathering, widened to include a community of old and new friends. And even though the guest towel that hangs in the bathroom states that "Guests of guests are not invited," in twenty years no one has ever been turned away.

Nowadays, on any given Monday you will find a group whose mean age is probably around seventy. The oldest (and a most interesting) person who attends regularly is ninety-three, but there are often teenagers in attendance, plus several people representing every decade in between. You never quite know who's going to show up or what's going to happen. Big Bird—yes, the real Big Bird—shows up on occasion, movie stars are not uncommon, state officials, including our favorite governor has shown up, local celebrities are frequent guests, and live music (some professional, some confessional) can be heard almost any week. But the best part of Monday Night Pizza is the welcome you get. No one is a stranger.

The research on aging well indicates that one of the strongest predictors of healthy longevity is going somewhere once a week where you are welcomed; where people are happy to see you. Monday Night Pizza fits the bill. Once Pat invited a friend to meet her at Monday Night Pizza, and by the time she arrived, this stranger had been there for no more than half an hour and had made five new friends already.

What holds Monday Night Pizza together? The hosts certainly have a lot to do with it. Judith, Steven, and Dr. Mac are such fascinating people, mainly because they have been in the game of life. Like the other people who are drawn to this group, they are interested in a wide range of subjects: politics, news, travel, family, relationships, ideas for better living, music, the arts, and literature. You can always get a great recommendation for your next book to read or trip to take at Monday Night Pizza. No matter whom you sit next to in this group, you can be guaranteed an interesting conversation.

What you will *not* find is people checking their cell phones or their computers or being interested only in talking about themselves, and you certainly will not hear complaints about aches and pains and medical problems. If you ask about someone's health, you'll get a reply, but there are so many more topics of interest to this group. Monday Night Pizza has become a community all its own—a community held together by fellowship, food, and fun, and it started all because a couple of parents wanted their son to come home more often!

The sense of belonging you get from being in a community is active, not passive; it is walking the walk, not just talking the talk, and there are so many ways to walk, get involved, and connect with the community. Here are some examples:

- **People bond around fun activities.** When your team wins, you high-five perfect strangers because you are all having fun at the same time. Being a fan makes you feel as though you belong; you feel connected to your team and the other fans. Within every community is some kind of team, and a team need supporters. How well do you support?

- **People bond around a common cause.** Friendships are made in the Sierra Club, book clubs, parent-teacher organizations, and the neighborhood cleanup. It is reassuring to knowing that when you get together, there will be an agenda as well as interests in common. What is your cause?

- **People bond around their passions.** These are activities that challenge and delight, like golfing, biking, dancing, painting, gardening, gaming, writing, and reading. For every passion, there's a group to support it and a way to get involved in a community around it. With the Internet, it's easy to access a community of people who share the same passion. What is your passion?

We could go on naming ways to become a part of a community, but the bottom line is that becoming part of a community requires involvement. To feel a connection and to experience a sense of community, you must invest your time and energy. Being in community means that you not only show up for the benefits, like the annual neighborhood picnic but also invest time in the maintenance and improvement of the neighborhood. Being in community means that you invest yourself.

Creating Intentional Community

Part of the research for this book included interviewing people who had moved away from loneliness, and as we listened to their responses, a pattern began to emerge. When asked, "How did you overcome the lonely times?" some cited helping a friend or making contact with family, but a significant majority of those interviewed said that their loneliness ultimately disappeared forever when they got involved in their communities, and especially when they put time and energy into activities that helped people they did not know, simply for the joy of helping. Many described a "helper's high" that made them feel connected and eliminated any feeling of loneliness.

The consensus of our interviews dovetailed nicely with the research that shows that a primary cause of loneliness today is loss of community. Just a few decades ago, the phrase loss of community would have been unthinkable, because living in community was the only option. When most people lived in small villages or towns, you saw the same individuals day after day, and the interdependent nature of life was evident.

No one had to ask for help when the need was obvious. If a family lost its barn in a fire, for instance, people came from miles around to rebuild. The grateful recipients knew that they would get a chance to return the favor when the next need occurred. There was dignity and reciprocity that reinforced the sense of community.

Today, however, half the world lives in huge cities, where you can go for days without seeing the same people, except at home and at work. In addition, families used to live in multigenerational households or at least in the same town; now the generations live apart, and often many miles apart. Despite this new way of life, our need to give and receive support is just as strong as it was years ago, so now we must be intentional in creating a sense of community wherever we live.

Helping one another is a matter of survival. Humans have evolved because of our willingness to form communities in which we combine resources and talents in a manner that helps the entire group. Helping creates a sense of belonging that cannot be attained any other way. Even young children spontaneously recognize the need for help.

One study took a toddler about eighteen months old and put him in a room with an adult, who was instructed to try to carry more books than he was able to manage. As the toddler watched, the man dropped the books and picked them up, only to drop them again. As the man struggled with his load, the toddler came to his aid. This scenario was repeated with several toddlers. Thus, even eighteen-month-old children recognized the need for help and spontaneously offered it.

Then the researchers changed the structure of the study. Again a toddler and a man were in a room, and the man was instructed to carry a heavy load of books. This time, however, he was instructed to throw down a book. This time no toddler in the study came to help. The toddlers knew the difference. When help was needed, they offered; when help was not needed, they didn't offer.

In yesterday's world, the need for help was obvious. Because a community was small, it was easy to detect a need and respond to it. As individuals provided assistance when and where it was needed, the sense of belonging to that community grew stronger. In today's world, it is not always clear who needs help, and there are even people who abuse the system that is designed to provide help to those who need it most. This fact should not stop us from offering assistance, however, not only because so many need it, but because we need to help just as much as others need our help. Investing in the betterment of the lives of others is a human survival strategy; we won't feel content without it.

Living without community involvement—whether the community is your neighborhood, your town, or the planet—creates a longing and a loneliness that can be alleviated only by your involvement.

If you want to experience living in community and deepen your sense of belonging, do something to help and improve the lives of others outside your intimate circle of friends and family. There are no hard and fast rules to finding a sense of community. However, one of the most potent experiences of community and belonging occurs when it is paired with compassion, support, caring, or kindness. When you lack community, you are lacking an active way to be compassionate or kind to others. It's so powerful that it will bring tears to your eyes and joy to your heart.

Pat was on the receiving end of a community act of kindness a couple of years ago. She had a blowout while driving seventy miles per hour, which was the legal speed limit on a particular four-lane highway in Texas. Although she was in one of the middle lanes, she managed to wrangle the car safely to the side of the road.

Once she had stopped, however, she was stranded in the middle of almost nowhere, and it was freezing cold. The only building within sight was a blacktop plant with one car parked outside, and as she approached the building a man came out and started to drive off. Pat flagged him down and asked if anyone was around whom she could pay to help her with her tire; she had tried to change it herself but couldn't figure out how to get to the spare tire. He said no, the weather was too cold to work and everyone had been sent home, and he drove off. (It rarely gets cold in Austin, so when it does, everything stops; people go home and hibernate for a day or two. It was also the beginning of the Thanksgiving holiday.) Pat went back to the road and continued to try to figure out how to access the tire that she knew was there but couldn't get to.

Then two men stopped, and despite the cold and the holiday, they stayed with her and figured out the intricacies of the secret compartment that holds the key that unlocks the compartment underneath the car where no one in their right mind would suspect that there's anything but dirt. Just getting to the tire took twenty to thirty minutes.

The men then replaced the tire, which took an hour in the freezing cold, and all was well. Pat wanted to pay them for their labor and their kindness, but when she tried, they adamantly refused, One of the men held up his hands in refusal and simply said, "Oh, no, this is what everyone should do for one another."

Now that was a connecting moment. Tears of joy filled both men's eyes and Pat's eyes, and the memory of that event is just as sweet as when it occurred.

It's comforting to live in a world where you find people like these two men; it makes you glad you belong. We know that you can cite many examples with the opposite outcome, but living in community requires that you can see the bright side of life. Otherwise, why would you want to belong?

In Dharamsala, it's easy to feel as though you belong. Even though the streets look different than our hometowns (Austin, Texas, and Lake Geneva, Wisconsin), from the moment we arrived we felt connected, because Dharamsala is a true worldwide community. The whole area is abuzz with people from the four corners of Earth who gather there for a common purpose: to do their part in making the world a better place. You can even get a contact high from the energy.

One day as we were sitting outside, eating at a restaurant across from our hotel, a bus drove up and about a dozen people got off. It's quite common to see buses in this area, so at first we gave it no notice. But then we became aware that the atmosphere had changed. There was a palpable sense of delight in the air—and it was coming from the people getting off the bus. It was as though a truckload of joy had pulled up, parked, and dumped its contents in front of us, and the joy began to infiltrate the air. The disembarking passengers were laughing and joking and almost skipping about as they unloaded gargantuan bags filled with clothing. The people didn't look anything like a group of tired travelers. Undoubtedly, their trip had been long, but you couldn't tell it by their enthusiasm.

We just sat in awe, watching them gleefully drag out more and more huge rectangular, zippered, suitcase-type plastic bags from the luggage compartment under the bus as well as from the passenger seating area. There were so many bags that we had to believe they had been sitting on them. Later we found out that this was a group from Australia who had been collecting clothing for the Tibetan Children's Village and had come all the way to India to hand-deliver the goods. It wasn't enough to send money, nor was it enough to bundle the T-shirts, pants, and coats; they wanted to meet the children and complete the circle of a wider community. Nelson Mandela would have approved!

Throughout the days we spent in Dharamsala, we kept running into these Aussies, and each time they were just as joyous. One day at lunch, two of them overheard us talking and deduced that we were in the area to meet with the Dalai Lama, so they came over to us and introduced themselves to us simply because we were going to meet him. They were awestruck at the possibility of meeting the Dalai Lama, but it was plain to see, from our perspective, that their experience of the helper's high was just as magnificent to them as meeting His Holiness was to us. Their energy had spread throughout the entire village; we're not sure that our energy did the same.

The Helper's High

Take it from the Aussies: the key to reaping the benefit of community is involvement. This doesn't mean that you have to travel to India or anywhere else. Getting involved can begin very close to home. The more time and effort you put in, the more you'll get back. If you belong to a neighborhood basketball league or even a loosely knit group that gathers once or twice a week, the more you show up, the more you will feel you belong when you get there. That's a no-brainer. Basketball, a movie matinee group, or a book club can be fun, but we are going to make a case for being a member of at least one community that provides a helping hand to others, because it is the quickest, most efficient, and most rewarding type of connection you can experience.

Helping is a survival skill. Humans aren't the strongest or the fastest species, but we have two advantages over other creatures: we have a big adaptable brain, and we help each other. One person doesn't have to know everything to survive, but you do need to know somebody who knows what you don't know to survive. We collaborate, we come to one another's aid, we work in teams, and we form kinship groups and communities. Because helping and cooperating are survival strategies (a baby cannot survive without a caregiver), the act of helping and working with others is reinforced by the release of dopamine, a feel-good neurotransmitter. We get a natural reward for helping others—for being generous, altruistic, or compassionate. When you feel this good, you cannot feel lonely.

There truly is a helper's high. In fact, Pat contends that it's much more reliable than the runner's high, because she has never felt the latter. Besides, how many runners do you see smiling? Jon disagrees; he has felt both the runner's high and the helper's high. Nonetheless, in *The Healing Power of Doing Good*, Allan Luks and Peggy Payne report that more than three thousand Americans found that when you help someone, there is a feeling of exhilaration and a burst of energy followed by a period of calmness and serenity that lasts several weeks. In addition, simply recalling the act of helping brings back the euphoric sensation.

There are numerous studies that validate the power and benefits of belonging to a community of volunteers. So along with any other community to which you belong, we're going to ask you to include at least one that involves helping.

How do you help? You can go about your life simply looking for opportunities to help—performing random acts of kindness, as the men who fixed Pat's tire did—and/or you can join a community that combines its efforts on a regular basis to render such services with a group impact. This is similar to what Buddhists call the *sangha*, a group of people who support one another in following the Middle Way, the path to enlightenment. The sangha is a community of helpers who are united by the common goal of compassionate living. They support one another and the causes they believe in.

The sangha, like other community groups, constitutes a powerful force. It's one thing for you as an individual to go along the riverbank and pick up trash, but if it is done regularly and with a group, you get not only a helper's high but also a profound sense of belonging to a community of helpers. There are few experiences which bond people together like combining their efforts for the good of others. It's also good for building your self-esteem. Being of service to others—using your talent to make your neighborhood, your community, or the world a better place—greatly improves your self-confidence. It reinforces your ability to make change happen not only in others' lives but also in your own.

When was the last time you experienced a helper's high? We are going to suggest that you make the helper's high a personal goal. You may want to strive for it once a day, once a week, or once a month—you decide. It's one of the best mood elevators on the planet. It can be a small act, like being patient in the grocery line when the cashier makes a mistake and holds up progress. A kind remark like "No problem, take your time" can mean a lot in a tense moment. Or it can be a bigger, more difficult act like forgoing your sumptuous Thanksgiving meal to serve food to the homeless at the nearby food bank. You decide.

Acts of community come in different forms and spread across a continuum from easy to difficult. You can give blood, donate used clothing, deliver Meals on Wheels, visit people in a nursing home, coach a team, help schoolchildren with reading, teach someone to read, train and volunteer for disaster relief, or participate in professional philanthropy with groups like Doctors Without Borders.

If none of these appeal to you, go to your city's website and find something to volunteer for there, or look more globally on the Internet for relief efforts and opportunities to provide aid. Don't be discouraged if your first few efforts fail to provide a helper's high. It might take some effort to find your niche, but you'll be comforted to know that you are moving in the right direction. The key is to hang in there and show up several times before you make a decision about whether to persist; the organization needs to know that it can depend upon you before the other volunteers will invest in you and welcome you fully.

"I Don't Have Time"

During our interviews, a response we heard time and again about getting involved in a community was "I don't have time." We are amused when people say this, because the truth is that we all have the same amount of time: twenty-four hours a day. It's how you decide to spend your time that differs. We believe that how you spend your time is directly related to how lonely you are. Activities that are not directly connected to others with regular face-to-face contact create a lack of community and increase loneliness. Let's look at how Americans spend their time and see where you might fall within this group.

Americans spend more of their waking time consuming media than doing anything else. People in the United States spend about nine and a half hours a day plugged in to some type of technology. They are plugged in and receiving stimulation from TV, radio, computers, phones, ebooks, iPads, game gadgets—you name it. They are receiving while they are eating, driving, walking, working; there's even a radio that works in the shower. And the consumers range from cradle to grave. Veteran journalist Bill Moyers has stated that children are being raised by appliances, not by people. We asked our nineteen-year-old friend Eddie, "Are you ever away from your phone?" With an incredulous expression, he replied, "No, it's always with me." We then asked, "Do you sleep with it nearby?" Without hesitation, he said, "It's on my bed."

Then we wanted to see if he fit the multitasking profile. "Do you ever find yourself listening to music, watching TV, texting, and surfing the Internet at the same time?" He shrugged and said, "Yes, and playing Xbox, too." Inordinate time spent engaged with technology can lead to suffering and loneliness if you become more and more removed from face-to-face connection.

It's not just young people who are plugged in most of the day. People in their fifties watch more TV than young people do, and other forms of media use is on the rise in this age group, too. Americans spend, on the average, almost three hours a day watching TV but only twenty minutes a day exercising and eight minutes a day volunteering or participating in religious or spiritual activities. Again, this leads to more disconnection from community and increased loneliness.

You might want to make the case that we are more connected now than ever before and that modern technology has made it easier to keep up with one another. Nevertheless, it is no substitute for face-to-face connection, and it leads to loneliness. Technology serves us best when it enhances, not replaces, personal relationships.

According to the latest American Time Use Survey (June 2010), during a 24-hour period, Americans slept 8.6 hours, spent 5.2 hours doing leisure and sports activities, worked for 3.7 hours (full time employed men worked 8.3 hours; full time employed women worked 7.5 hours), and spent 1.7 hours doing household activities. The remaining 4.8 hours were spent in a variety of other activities, including eating and drinking, attending school, and shopping.

Wow. Shopping made the Time Use Survey in the same category as eating and drinking. Think about that. Shopping made the list, but volunteering didn't, and we are not talking about shopping for necessities like groceries and gas. How long does it take to pick up food for the week? Sport shopping—shopping for the fun of it—gives you a short-lived burst of pleasure; some call it "retail therapy." This type of shopping, which leads only to short-term pleasure, takes more of our time than investing in community, which leads to long-term happiness.

Why are we picking on shopping, you might be wondering, when there's leisure and sports taking up a whopping 5.2 hours per day? If your goal is to never be lonely again, sports and leisure have a greater chance of alleviating loneliness than shopping does. Shopping for pleasure has inherent flaws: it requires a repeat performance to make you feel good, because the half-life of enjoyment is so short; it fuels the work-and-spend cycle that adds stress to people's lives; and it creates guilt because it constitutes such a waste of time and money, both of which could be spent in far more rewarding ways.

Shop Till You Drop

You've probably seen the sign "When the going gets tough, the tough go shopping." Even though you might say this with tongue in cheek, there is some truth to it. Shopping can be a pick-me-up. Women have a reputation for doing the most sport shopping, but research doesn't support this bias. Men shop just about as much as women do, but they tend to call it "collecting" instead of shopping. It doesn't matter what you call it; spending time shopping might give you short-term pleasure, but it won't give you long-term happiness, nor will it keep loneliness at bay. Much of the time spent shopping is self-centered, not other-centered.

When you listed your core values for who you are, did "shopper" make the list? When you are dead, do you want to be remembered for your shopping? "I don't know if he loved me, but he had a lot of stuff." Or "She didn't have time to volunteer at my school, but she kept the closets full." On your deathbed, do you think you'll be saying, "I wish I had shopped more"? Are you spending precious time and energy shopping that could be spent in far more rewarding ways for you and others?

The lure of shopping is so great that we do it at all hours of the day and night. We make time for it regardless of our other commitments. It's not that we need more things; Americans lead the world in the accumulation of stuff. We have more stuff than we have time to use or room to store, yet we still spend a significant amount of our precious time gathering more. We pay an average of $100 per square foot just to heat, air-condition, and house our stuff. One-third of us can't park the car in the garage because the garage is full of our stuff—even though the average garage size has almost doubled and in the last decade there has been a 60 percent increase in the number of three-car garages.

A mere twenty years ago, each American had one closet with one rail in it. Now we have closet organization systems, and it's a multi-billion-dollar business. More and more people are even turning to outside help to acquire more room to house more stuff. The United States now has 2.5 billion square feet of storage space away from the home. That's more than 7 square feet for every man, woman, and child. It's now physically possible for every American to fit, standing up, in our storage spaces!

We are focusing here on shopping and stuff because it's a fact that lonely and unhappy people shop more and accumulate more stuff. It makes you wonder which came first, the chicken or the egg. Do lonely people shop more, or does excessive shopping make you lonely? Millions of people are caught up in the work-and-spend cycle that is a breeding ground for loneliness. "I work hard and therefore deserve the reward I get from spending," people rationalize. The problem with this thinking is that the reward translates only into short-term pleasure not long-term happiness. Happiness comes from using your particular talents for the good of society or to help others. When you take an active part in making your community better for everyone, you invest in long-term satisfaction and a connection with others that eliminates loneliness.

On some level it makes sense that unhappy and lonely people go shopping; after all, it does get you out and give you at least a moment of pleasure. But the pleasure exhausts itself in the moment; to feel good, you have to keep shopping and keep consuming. As humans, we lose interest quickly in a new purchase because of a phenomenon known as *hedonic adaptation*. New pleasure quickly becomes the norm—

and thus no longer pleasurable. We have to keep shopping for it to be pleasurable. The short-lived high we get from a new cosmetic or a camouflage koozie dissolves into normality almost overnight.

We tire even sooner of a new gadget or an item of clothing that we don't need, but we still hang on to it. Storage bins are full of things that we paid too much for, so now we would feel too guilty or foolish if we let them go. Stuff suffocates our lives by taking our time and attention. It clutters our homes and sucks the life out of our days. We can't invite friends over because our homes are cluttered with stuff; we can't take time to socialize because we've got to tend to our stuff. Stuff has become a surrogate for social exchange, whether it's technological stuff or just simple stuff. Regardless of how much stuff you have or don't have, accumulating, shopping, and collecting will never give you enough pleasure or anywhere near the exhilaration you will feel from a helper's high.

If you are a collector of stuff or a sport shopper, think about how your life might be different if you invested your time and money into community activities that directly improve the lives of others. If you shopped only for necessities and not for sport, and you applied the time and energy you saved to investing in your community, you would be taking some important steps toward never being lonely again.

As we have mentioned, the trip to India changed us. When we returned home, life looked different, our priorities were clearer, our core values were more relevant, and the vagaries of our lives were more visible.

Pat's Stuff

When I returned from India, the reentry was initially like most other times I had been away on a lengthy trip. There was the usual collection of mail, e-mails, phone calls, wilted plants, and relationships to catch up with. But as the days and weeks passed, I felt more and more incongruent as I spent time keeping up with what had become nonessential parts of my life. I hadn't been living in an extravagant fashion by most U.S.

standards, but I realized that maintaining my current residence required more time, money, and energy than my core values allowed. To keep it up I would have to work longer and harder and take precious time from the more meaningful goals I had now set for myself. I had tasted the joy of another way of life, and I knew it was time for me to show up, pay attention, comprehend, and realign my life so that I was behaving more congruently.

With this knowledge in mind, I did the unconscionable: I put my house on the market. This might not sound like a big deal to some people, but since early adulthood I had made my home my haven. During my childhood, home was not a safe place, so I made a vow to myself that I would change that when I grew up. As an adult I made my home as beautiful, comfortable, hospitable, and nurturing as possible. I welcomed guests, visitors, and strays; I hosted parties, celebrations, and family gatherings, and I enjoyed every minute of it. Now I was willfully walking away from that option, at least in the customary style.

(Unbeknown to me, Jon and his wife had also put their house on the market and were in the process of downsizing!)

I put my home up for sale thinking that I'd have time to make the emotional transition slowly. Wrong! Within two days I had two offers. In addition, both offers came with a request: the buyers wanted my house with everything in it. I mean *everything*, from the artwork to the salt and pepper shakers (which I had brought home from St. John in the Virgin Islands). I was somewhat prepared to sell my house, but the thought of selling most of my belongings took my breath away, so I said no way.

But then I looked at the idea with a more mindful attitude. I stepped into a world where I just walked away from the stuff. I decided that I would take the personal items and memorabilia, but I'd leave the stuff that I could easily replace if I ever needed to. (I admit that the thought of getting to shop and acquire new stuff was somewhat appealing.) So I let it all go.

It would be difficult for me to explain how exhausting and time-consuming it was to dismantle umpteen years of accumulation; the last 10 percent grew in quantum proportions. For example, I thought that my garage was pretty clear, yet even though I was one of the nearly 70 percent of people who can fit the car in the garage, dismantling the stuff in my garage took at least two weeks.

It was all very tough physically and emotionally, but I'd do it again in a heartbeat, because on the other side was a life free from stuff, free from the worries of housing and maintaining stuff that stood in the way of a mindful life.

I did not own my own home again for three years. I was not sure what I wanted to do, in terms of acquiring a living space, so it made more sense to "don't just do something; stand there." Meanwhile, my daughter Kathleen was trying to figure out how she could continue to stay at home with her then seven-year-old daughter, Katie. Although her husband, Devin, has a good job, they really needed a second income to be able to stay in their big home.

We had talked for years about combining resources and living more mindfully, so we decided that this was a good time to do it. I had lived alone and didn't like it, and I didn't want to have a roommate, not even a good friend. I just wanted to relax for a while, to have time to think and take the pressure off. They were pleased to have a familiar and supportive renter, and I was happy to have a loving place to live. Once I simplified my life, I immediately had more time for friends, family, work, hobbies, and volunteering and my experience with the helper's high began to increase.

Your Time Is Your Wealth

Granted, walking away from your home and renting a room from your daughter for three years is extreme, but the idea poses some important questions: Is your lifestyle conducive to your core values?

Does your lifestyle, and the way you spend your time, allow you to be in community in the ways you desire and need? Is your life focused on consumption or connection? Which comes first for you, consuming (media, technology, stuff) or connecting with your community?

Recent studies of consumption and happiness show that people are happier when they spend money on experiences instead of material objects. Spending money supporting the arts, taking cooking lessons, or learning to speak Spanish will make you happier than buying stuff, and it will be an investment in your community. Entertainment, vacations, and sports can increase contentment as well as community and social bonds. Why not use your money to strengthen your bonds to the wider community by going on a mission trip, such as helping to build wells for safe water in Haiti? Your time is your wealth; how you spend it will determine how lonely you are.

Right Effort and Circles of Community

How do you begin to improve your connection to community? The Dalai Lama talks about the concept of right effort, which has to do with how you use your time and your energy. One of the reasons we have focused on time spent shopping or surfing the Internet is to help you evaluate how you are using your time and your energy. If you look back at your core values in Chapter 3, you will find guidance for right effort. Your core values serve as a guide for how to use your resources. Included in the concept of right effort is the act of avoiding activities that distract you from your best self and, instead, focusing your energy on activities that lead to congruence with your core values.

From His Holiness's perspective, right effort has to include acts of kindness, generosity, service to others, and munificence. Most likely your list of core values includes some characteristic related to benevolent acts. To strengthen your ties to community and avoid the loneliness that comes from the longing for belonging, you have to extend your benevolent acts beyond your intimate borders. Your actions have to include more people than those who are closest to you. You must reach outside your close circle of friends and family to make contact with community.

The Dalai Lama teaches that right effort includes self-discipline as well as benevolent acts. Having the restraint to keep your actions in line with your core values is a big part of right effort. So how do you start?

Let's begin at home. During our interviews, many people said, "How can I help other people? I hardly have time to help myself." Many people described the limitless number of jobs awaiting them at home. When questioned further, many of these same people admitted that their homes were too big and too full to manage. The overwhelming nature of their most intimate environment—the home—was taking an enormous amount of time and energy. No wonder there are so many reality TV shows about cleaning up your home.

So, for a moment, think about where you live and where you sleep. Does it exemplify self-discipline? What does the inside of your home look like? Is it conducive to easy living? Does it give you energy or take energy? Are you comfortable sharing it with others? Do you have the right amount of stuff? Do you have time to use all the stuff you have? Is any of it broken or outdated? Are you saving clothes for some day in the future when you think you might fit into them again? Trust us on this one: if you lose weight, you are going to want new clothes. Besides, even people in Santa Fe don't wear the Santa Fe style anymore.

Even if you have lots of good stuff, think about it this way: there are people who need that stuff. Earlier, Jon told his story about going to buy clothes to wear to see the Dalai Lama and ending up with pajamas. When Pat's luggage was lost and she went out and bought her red tunic and pants, her shopping trip was an adventure, too. The group had been spending a couple of days in Delhi before leaving for Dharamsala, and the hotel that Jhampa had chosen for us was located in a busy retail district. So Pat set out walking in the hope of finding some appropriate Indian clothing. She went to store after store, with no luck. There were bookstores, CD stores, food stores, and bicycle stores, but no clothing stores anywhere.

Finally, she asked someone, "Where can I find clothing to buy?" She was directed to a huge market about three blocks away; sure enough, it was full of clothes—but all Western-style clothing. There were piles and piles of jeans, shirts, sweaters, skirts, and blouses, all used and all Western. People were pushing, shoving, and crowding while digging frantically through the piles of used clothing from the United States. "This is what people want," said a salesman. "They don't want the typical Indian wear."

If you haven't had the pleasure of dropping off a load of stuff that you don't need to Goodwill or a local donation center, do yourself—and others—a favor. There are people in need waiting for you to part with much of the stuff that is taking time and energy from your life.

What does the condition of your home say about who you are? Does it say "I am a person with self respect" or "I am a person who deserves a comfortable place to live"? You send a message to other people based on your internal beliefs about yourself. Improving your self-esteem by making your home more comfortable can translate into a more comfortable image that you present to the outside world. We like to be around people who increase our comfort levels. Improving your comfort level with yourself improves your comfort level with others. Making positive changes in your relationships with community may begin right where you live.

Now let's take a step outside your home. Think of the community that exists outside your front door. Whether you live in an apartment, a condominium, a single-family dwelling, or mobile home, ask yourself the following: Do you take care of your home in a way that improves the neighborhood? What does the outside of your home say about your commitment to the community? Whether you have a holiday wreath on the door, a welcome mat, or a junk-free yard, does your home say, "I respect the community where I live"? What does the outside of your home say about your sense of self-discipline and benevolence, your investment in the community?

Your sense of community exists in direct proportion to the effort you put into it. Without involvement; without investing your time and energy, you will feel alienated, distanced from the very environment that supports you. The loneliness for belonging can be eradicated by involvement; even sweeping the front sidewalk is an investment, a connection to the wider circle of life. What if you decided to improve where you live, just a little? Your improvement would make a difference to you as well as to others.

It may seem like a stretch to think that cleaning up your home can lead to less loneliness in your life, but think about it this way: When the Dalai Lama talks about right effort, he is referring to how we use our time and energy. He urges us to move toward benevolence, toward making life better instead of expecting life to better us. People ask us all the time, "Where do I start?" Our answer here has been to start at home—begin with self-respect—and then move outward. For some, this means making the home and the immediate community cleaner, safer, and friendlier.

There is a strong subculture in this country that consists of parents who volunteer to clean the neighborhood around schools. They pick up trash, remove graffiti, and apply fresh paint—all to show that they care for their children's safety as well as their education. Studies have found that a clean environment decreases crime. Vandals and criminals are less likely to congregate in a cared-for area. Would you rather live in a clean and orderly neighborhood or a dirty and messy one? Community involvement has many benefits beyond the obvious.

During the week leading up to our audience with the Dalai Lama, we did some hiking in the surrounding area, and one particular trail led us past a weaver and her small display of items for sale. We were impressed not only with her wares but also with the lovely flowers she had planted in a small plot in front of her home. As we talked with her and admired her flowers, she extended an invitation for us to come inside and see where she lived. We were all very curious but didn't want to impose, so at first we politely refused, but she insisted. We had the impression that she knew we were interested, so she made it easy for us by leading the way through the low-hung door and into her one-room dwelling. Her husband was seated inside on a mattress that served as a bed and a couch. There was a small fire built right on the floor with a teapot hanging above the flames by a wire frame. She offered tea as he nodded his head for us to sit. We sat, drank tea, and spoke few words, but we felt a tremendous sense of community.

When was the last time you offered someone a cup of tea? Have you widened the circle of your community to include others? How do you invest in your neighborhood? Do you know your neighbors? Have you introduced yourself? Have you taken some cookies to the new tenants next door or extended a helping hand? You might be thinking, *I don't have the energy* or *I just don't feel like it.* If you feel resistance, feel the feeling and acknowledge your resistance, but do the right thing anyway. If you are lonely, "follow your feelings" can be bad advice. You often have to act *despite* your feelings. Feel the feeling, but act according to your core values. Acts of benevolence improve your feelings. If you want to feel better, act better.

When Pat left for India, she let her neighbors know that she would be gone for three weeks. This was a common practice shared among the three or four closest houses. When she returned from India, she was glad to see that everything was intact and working; as wonderful as travel is, it's always delightful to come home. A couple of days after her return, her closest neighbors, Beth and Chuck, told her about a little incident that had occurred in her absence.

About a week after Pat had left the country, they noticed water seeping down along the foundation of her house. On inspection they realized that it was getting wetter and wetter, so they used the garage code Pat had given them to go in and check it out. On entering the garage, they saw that the hot-water tank had burst and the water was running through the garage, out into the foundation, and even into the sitting room inside the house. The carpet in that room was soaked. Imagine the mess. Once they ascertained the problem, Beth and Chuck, on their own, replaced the hot-water tank, lifted the carpet, and put a dehumidifier and a hot fan in the room to dry it all off. Once it had dried, they reattached the carpet and repositioned all the furniture.

Pat didn't know that anything had been done until a couple of days after her return because they wanted her to have a little time to rest. That's the kind of neighbors to have! These neighbors were not even friends that she hung out with and socialized with; they were just very private, respectful, neighborly people who take community seriously.

Only you know how you need to connect to your community.

Jon acknowledges that his community has changed over the years. "Community now consists of the parents of our children's friends, the church community, our work colleagues, our running buddies, people we go to Starbucks with, and even grade school and high school friends. My friendships also continue to change. I don't see some people anymore because they have died, moved away, or found new associations.

"My immediate community is my family and my friends Tom, Jeffrey, Phil, and Hank. I maintain contact with many friends in Thailand, grade school and high school friends through annual reunions, and many colleagues through professional meetings and numerous projects, such as this book. My friend Jeffrey and I collaborate on a book every year as a means to stay connected. We are now on book number nine."

Jon chooses to participate in the global community by volunteering his time and his talents around the world to write, teach, and develop materials for people to use to improve their lives. At least once a year he travels to Thailand, where he donates his time and his talent for personal improvement programs and experiences. But the most impactful way that Jon exercises his sense of community (what Alfred Adler might call social interest) is to connect people who have resources to people who have a need for these resources. Behind the scenes, almost anonymously, Jon networks people all over the world, connecting them in ways in which few people are aware. He's always on the lookout for someone who has a talent and others who need that talent. He quietly yet powerfully gets the right people in community with one another. He is a community builder extraordinaire—it just seems to be in his DNA.

Exercise 16: **With and Without Community**

The purpose of this exercise is to give you a taste of life with and without community. It begins, like the other meditations, with relaxation and focus.

As you sit comfortably with an erect posture, begin to focus on your breath. Become aware of the air coming in and the air going out. Take the time you need to simply focus on your breath. As thoughts come, let them float by and let them go, then return to focusing on your breath.

Once you have relaxed and are focusing on your breath, imagine yourself alone where you sit. No one is near you. You are all alone. No one can hear you, no one can see you, and no one knows you are there. Be aware that there is no one within a block of you. Now imagine that there is no one within a mile of you, then two miles, then three. There is stone silence, no human sounds. Just sit with the awareness that no one is nearby and no one is coming. You are alone for one day, then two days, then a week.

On the first day of the second week there is a knock at your door. You open the door and a stranger says, "We need your help. Would you please come?" You follow the guide and are led to a community of people.

"We need all kinds of assistance," the guide says. "We need your ability to listen, we need your creative talents, we need your physical strength, we need your encouragement, we need your objective eye, we need your technical knowledge, we need your company, we need your experience, we need your humor, we need your nurturing, and we need your healing presence."

As your guide is presenting the menu of needs, you see the exact way in which you can help. It's very clear. You move forward and begin to help, and as you are helping you notice the feeling of connection and community. The feeling energizes you, supports you, and fills you with happiness and contentment. You lose track of time; your body has renewed strength. You get the sense that "This is exactly what I'm supposed to be doing. This is who I am."

Stay with this meditation, and as you follow your breath again, remind yourself of the power of community and the way it can transform lives, including yours.

Exercise 17: Connected Helping

Find a comfortable place where you can sit peacefully and quietly. As you sit, begin to notice your breath. Notice that you can breathe slowly and deeply. You can inhale and exhale freely and easily. As we have learned, the more we can reach out and help others, the deeper the connection we feel to the community. As you exhale, quietly say the word *helping*, and as you inhale, say the word *connected*. If your mind wanders, gently bring it back.

This activity is best done for ten days for fifteen to thirty minutes each day. After the initial practice, use it whenever you find yourself experiencing loneliness and are unsure of what to do.

Deciding How to Become Involved

How serious are you about belonging to your community, whether it is your neighborhood, your town, your country, or the world at large? You belong only when your beliefs are bolstered by your behavior. What does belonging mean to you? Are you where you want to be? If not, what do you need to change? What action would give you a helper's high?

Only you can decide how to be more involved in your community. There are the traditional routes: philanthropic organizations such as food banks, Habitat for Humanity, homeless shelters, halfway houses, or Hospice. Churches, synagogues, and mosques provide groups with organized outreach. Our friend Mary Ann volunteers through her church to teach Friendship International, which is a group experience designed to help spouses, usually wives of graduate students at colleges and universities who are migrating to the United States learn about

American culture. She uses her cooking talents to educate others on how to utilize the food resources in their new communities.

You, too, can use your hobbies and interests as a vehicle for helping and investing in your community. Our friend Jeffrey, while visiting Nepal, learned that girls who did not have money for school were sold into sexual slavery. Jeffrey raised money and created Empower Nepali Girls. Each winter he and many of the benefactors travel to Nepal to present the scholarships in person. A few dollars can save a life. Jeffrey's actions have saved hundreds already. Check it out at http://Empower NepaliGirls.org.

There are so many ways to get involved, and sometimes it's as simple as following your interests. You can support an animal shelter if you are an animal lover, participate in the annual bird species count if you are a bird watcher, or clean up a hiking trail if you are a hiker. A bicyclist we know spends one weekend a month offering free bike repair on the biking trail. Schools, nursing homes, and hospitals always need help.

Your job or professional skills may be of use for volunteering also. One of our therapist friends volunteers at a community college to provide free counseling services to students once a week. An acquaintance volunteers his business-consulting knowledge at a domestic violence shelter, helping the staff to streamline its administrative practices.

Community involvement, investing in benevolent acts outside your immediate friends and family, is a fast track away from loneliness. When you feel you belong because you are invested, no matter where you are in the world, you will never be lonely again.

6

Are My Talents Utilized in Meaningful Work?

ALL LABOR THAT UPLIFTS HUMANITY HAS DIGNITY
AND IMPORTANCE AND SHOULD BE UNDERTAKEN
WITH PAINSTAKING EXCELLENCE.

—Martin Luther King Jr.

Do you get the sense that the work you do uplifts humanity? Do your daily tasks, the ways you use your time and your energy, have dignity and importance? If your talents lie dormant and your efforts do not support your core values, your personal connections, or your purpose, then your work will not be meaningful. Spiritual, sociological, and psychological studies tell us that meaningful work is vital to avoid emptiness, isolation, and a life unfulfilled.

Alfred Adler was one of the first psychologists to remind us that no individual possesses all the requisite knowledge to be totally self-sufficient; therefore, we must all work to sustain life. We are born into dependency—in our early years, others work to feed, clothe, and shelter us—but this dependency extends well beyond childhood. We depend on one another to produce the goods and services that are required to meet the multitude of needs in today's complex society.

Teachers cannot build their own homes, design their own cars, grow their own food, and still have time to teach. Physicians cannot supply their own water, make their own clothes, concoct the medicines they prescribe, and simultaneously practice medicine. Farmers cannot dig for iron ore, forge the tools and equipment they need, and still find time to work the land. Parents cannot build the necessary roads and bridges, provide police and fire protection, and still have time to provide love and support for their children.

No one can do it all, but each person can do a part to create and sustain the cycle of life. When talents are combined in meaningful work, each person is necessary and fulfilled. Isolation and emptiness cease to exist when we are connected by the cycle of life. When you are not part of this connection, loneliness creeps in. Regardless of how you go about it, making a contribution by applying your abilities builds a connection between you and the greater part of society.

If you don't have something to do on a regular basis that puts your abilities to use, it's as though part of you were missing. You are disconnected from the cycle of contribution that sustains society. You experience a void of responsibility. You get lonely for the feeling of accomplishment that comes with a job well done. If you are employed at a job, if your talents are not being utilized in a meaningful manner, either at work or after work, you won't feel very relevant. You are more likely to feel incongruent, unfulfilled, and insecure, because you are missing the sense of bonding that comes with contributing as others are contributing. Using your talents in a productive way connects you to your sense of authenticity, dignity, and value.

If you haven't taken the time to think about how your talents are used in meaningful work, we recommend that you do it now. Sometimes just simple awareness makes your work more meaningful. You may be the person who helps to maintain the water supply in your community, which keeps your fellow citizens healthy, happy, and able to live productive lives. You may work with software that enables people to stay in touch with one another or perform better in their work. Or you may take care of children, supporting the future citizens of tomorrow's world. Whether your talents contribute to the cycle of life in large or small ways matters not; it's your attitude that creates meaning.

We saw this meaningful attitude toward work in the hours before dawn on a side street in Dharamsala. We had been in India only two days and were still adjusting to the time difference (which explains why four of us had awoken and were out walking the streets in the dark). Even without daylight it was clear that we were somewhere else (outside our normal environment), because before we encountered a person, we encountered a cow. There it was, rummaging through the trash that had been thrown on the street for the cleaners to pick up.

As a protected animal in India, the cow is often treated as a member of the family, but there are no leash laws for this family pet, so you are just as likely to find one in the middle of a superhighway or on the sidewalk as in a farmyard. Cows roam about feeding on garbage and anything else they can find. On this particular morning we were excited to see a cow. We had arrived at our destination and were ready to begin the next step of our adventure, so there we were, all dressed up and with no one to talk to—but the cow wasn't interested.

We had strolled most of the streets in town, when we finally came to a narrow one-way alley and heard voices off in the distance. Down at the very end of the alley, a dim light glowed from an open storefront, so we headed off in that direction. We came upon a tiny shop about five feet wide and eight feet deep, with two short benches to sit on and a man behind a small counter of sorts, stirring a pot of chai tea.

"Namaste," he greeted us, "come in and sit." We hesitated and felt a little guilty, because once the four of us sat down, there was nowhere for anyone else to sit, and by now, customers were coming in a steady stream. You could tell they were regulars, because when they came to the shop, they automatically stepped inside, but then they paused when they saw a group of Westerners hogging all the space. Two members of our group drank their tea and left, but the other two of us continued to sit there, fascinated by the morning ritual that was unfolding.

Amol, the man who was serving and selling the tea, spoke little English but was quite fluent in friendliness. Our guess was that the townspeople came in for his cheerfulness as much as the chai. He joked and laughed and made others laugh. Amol might have had many other talents, but at that moment he was using his talent for cheering others in the morning. He was an important part of the cycle of life in Dharamsala.

Whether you consider your talents large or small, think about the following: Are they being utilized in meaningful work—that is, work that supports your core values, builds connection with others, and fits into a purposeful life? Are you simply working so you won't starve, or does your work have further meaning?

Orientations Toward Work

Positive-psychology researcher Amy Wrzesniewski describes three distinct orientations that people have toward work:

1. **Work as a job.** Work is a source of income, enabling desired out-comes and activities outside work. A job is held to support a family or to fund one's hobbies. Job satisfaction comes primarily from the income earned.
2. **Work as a career.** Work is a ladder, a progression toward greater pay, status, and responsibility. Job satisfaction comes primarily from continuing advancement. A person who sees work as a career will often dedicate extraordinary amounts of time and energy to the work, considering that to be the temporary cost of future gain.
3. **Work as a calling.** Satisfaction is derived from the work itself. The person feels called to do the work, based on inner drives and the sense that the work derives from an inner or a higher direction.

Let's look at these three categories from the perspective that mean-ingful work wards off loneliness.

Work as a Job

Sociological studies show that a large percentage of workers around the world can't wait until their jobs are over at the end of the day. Time on the job may be hard, boring, or simply a bad match for their skills. The employees may be dissatisfied with the pay or the long hours that are required.

For example, the average worker in the United States commutes fifty minutes a day, and many spend far more time than this traveling to and from work. Commuting is seen as a necessary evil in today's work culture, but people usually overestimate the trade-offs. They travel farther to earn more money, acquire more material goods, and gain more prestige, but this may be at the expense of their social connections, their hobbies, and their health, all of which are directly related to loneliness.

Studies show that commuters are generally much less satisfied with their lives than noncommuters. According to the University of Zurich's Institute for Empirical Research in Economics, a commuter who travels one hour one way would have to make 40 percent more than his or her current salary to be as fully satisfied with life as a noncommuter is. Commuting is associated with elevated blood pressure, musculoskeletal disorders, and increased hostility. Furthermore, for every ten minutes of commuting time, one's social connections are cut by 10 percent. Robert Putnam, author of *Bowling Alone: The Collapse and Revival of American Community*, points out that commuter math isn't friendly when it comes to loneliness.

One couple, Jason and Jessica, recently did the math on commuting and made some drastic changes to increase their contact time with their two kids, Robbie and Kirsten, ages ten and twelve, respectively. Jessica had been getting up at 5:00 AM to commute to a job near Washington, D.C. The pay was great, but the commute took three hours out of each day. That left Jason with the task of getting the kids off to school every day, and it left the kids alone at home in the late afternoon, sometimes for up to two hours. Jessica left before daylight and returned home after dark every day that she worked.

After examining their lifestyle from the point of view of core values, connections, and purpose, they decided that it was far more meaningful to sacrifice a little money for a lot more quality time. Jessica found a job working three days a week for twelve hours, which left her free to be home with the family four days a week instead of two. Her work took on meaning as she strengthened her connections to her family and her core values.

People who practice work as a job are not necessarily condemned to loneliness. Such labor can provide the means to create a meaningful life with its own rewards. Time on the job may require tremendous commitment, but at the end of the workday, a meaningful reward awaits. These people go home to their families and their friends and enjoy the fruits of their labor. Their work connects them to the cycle of life by making a contribution toward housing, food, utilities, clothes, health care, and entertainment—all for the people they love.

Their talents include tenacity, dependability, and sacrifice as well as the skills of the job. Time after work may also afford the opportunity to apply a special talent for music or some other creative endeavor. Working at a job may provide free time to complete life's chores so that your partner, your roommate, or your kids can afford to utilize their talents in direct services such as volunteer work.

If you view work as a job, does it have meaning? If not, what changes do you need to make?

Work as a Career

When your work takes on the form of a career, it focuses on utilizing a set of skills and talents over the years. A career usually consists of many jobs in a related area and is seen as a long-term endeavor. A job can become less satisfying over time unless your talents are being applied, whereas a career most often involves the development of your talents. Developing your talents and gaining mastery is intrinsically rewarding. In addition, employers who offer work with a career path are motivated to improve the skills of the employees. The worker benefits from learning and developing skills; the employer benefits from having a more satisfied, productive employee. A career is rewarding, because it challenges and educates you. Work as a job can challenge and educate you, too, but most people see a job as a means to an end, whereas they see their career as an end in itself.

A career also encompasses the lifestyle that goes with it, because by its nature a career will often require more of your time than a job does. As Wrzesniewski states, those on a career path see work as a progression toward greater pay, status, and responsibility, with satisfaction gained from continuing advancement. A career path can be seductive, for the monetary rewards are great, but it is important to keep in mind that the time investment in career advancement is frequently extraordinary and seldom as temporary as one might wish.

Career experts are consistent in emphasizing the importance of planning. We urge you to be just as consistent by asking yourself the following: Are my talents being utilized in meaningful work? Is my work in line with my core values? Does it support my connections to the important people in my life? Does it lead to a life of purpose?

Work as a Calling

Some people get paid to do what they believe they were put on Earth to do. They feel called to the work by God, destiny, intuition, fortune, or natural talent. These individuals just know that they are doing what they are supposed to be doing. Some people practice a calling without being paid in money; the work is gratification enough. The jobs they hold enable them to work at the calling. For instance, a state employee we know works at his job so he can dedicate time, money, and energy to his calling: maintaining a model airplane association. This brings happiness and camaraderie to thousands of people around the world.

Alfred Adler believed that mentally healthy people possess social interest and therefore are concerned about helping others through their work and generosity. That is, healthy people are connected and seem to understand the interconnection of humanity; they know that life is not about "me or them"; it's about "us." Adler believed that it was crucial for healthy people to have socially useful ways to fit into the world. Humans are social animals; when they bond, they flourish, and when they are isolated, they do not. As Jon and his coauthors wrote in *Adlerian Therapy*, "Thousands of years of evolution have left their mark. People still need to contribute. As their contribution to the general welfare of the group increases, so does their personal success."

It's easy to underestimate the importance of work in reference to a meaningful life, but research won't let us. For example, the *Economic Journal* followed 130,000 people for several decades and found that if you go a full year without work, the recovery time from that loss is greater than the recovery time from losing a spouse. Work in general, and meaningful work in particular, is that important.

Job stress is a serious issue, however. Stress produces cortisol, and the prolonged release of cortisol depresses your immune system, making you more susceptible to disease. Cortisol release also raises your blood pressure and your blood sugar level, which can cause more health complications. When we are unemployed, underemployed, or employed in ways that oppose our values, we feel stress, which can lead to disconnection and loneliness. It seems that we don't belong to or fit in the world. When we spend time at work that lacks meaning, we feel useless and unimportant, and so we frequently act that way.

How Work Can Contribute to Loneliness

There are four basic ways that your work can contribute to loneliness: if it is not using your talents, if it lacks meaning, if it involves what we call golden handcuffs, and if it involves overworking. Let's explore each of these in turn.

What Are My Talents?

One of the greatest challenges to meaningful work is a lack of clarity about your talents. It's not uncommon to hear people say that they have no talent. If this is your point of view, let us assure you that everyone has some innate capabilities. You might not think of certain abilities you hold as talents because the term *talent* is often reserved for skills like sports, singing, painting, writing, acting, or designing. But a talent is simply the ability to do something well—a much broader definition.

A talent is something you enjoy doing. You even look forward to doing it. Using a talent or an ability gives you pleasure and energy; it holds your interest. It's not too difficult to stay at it, because it's engaging. It's important to your mental health and happiness to do what you do well and to focus on the joy others receive from what you do. Sometimes you are born with a particular talent, and sometimes a talent is developed. You can develop a talent in many ways. Studies of famous athletes and performers have determined that these people possessed two characteristics that helped them to develop their talents: the ability to take feedback, or coaching, and the willingness to practice. Are you the type of person who is willing to listen to others and put in hours of practice?

According to Malcolm Gladwell in *Outliers: The Story of Success*, the mastery of any activity comes with time. He states that it takes 10,000 hours to master a skill set, whether it be hockey or a foreign language. Gladwell defines success as meaningful work, and for work to be meaningful, in Gladwell's definition, it must have complexity, autonomy, and a clear relationship between effort and reward. Meaningful work is hard work with people who encourage us and mentor us and work that provides opportunities to use our talents.

It is important to note that meaning comes long before mastery in the world of work. This means that you begin to get the benefit as soon as you put in some effort. Getting better at a task is intrinsically rewarding and will add quality to your life. Mastery takes time, but it is time that will feed energy back into your core values, your connections, and your purpose in life. So it is never too late to begin to develop the talents that lie dormant, waiting for your attention.

A challenge to finding our talent sometimes occurs when we don't get the talent we think we want. Pat would like to have a great singing voice that would entertain and make people happy. Jon thinks being a U.S. senator would be fun, because he'd get to make decisions that improve people's lives. Jon probably has a much better chance of being a senator than Pat has of being a singer, but, fortunately, these fantasies don't get in the way of their happiness; they are grateful for the abilities they have. One way to set yourself up for loneliness is to pine away for talents you don't have instead of focusing on and being grateful for the capabilities you do have.

Sometimes talents aren't what they appear to be. For example, Pat and Jon do not believe that they have a talent for writing. Pat calls herself an author, not a writer. Jon says that he's someone who writes, but he's not a writer. Writing doesn't come easily for either of them, nor do they particularly enjoy it. Pat's talent, which is expressed in writing, is the ability to take complex information and put it into simple terms. She loves research, learning, teaching, and helping, and writing is simply the means by which she expresses these talents. Jon, too, enjoys integrating different ideas and making the complex useful, and he, too, uses writing as a means by which to sort through and express his thoughts and ideas.

How have the two of us published numerous books when we don't particularly enjoy writing or have talent for it? Jon realized the importance of writing in academia; he saw it as part of the job. Teaching is one of Jon's talents; in fact, he's passionate about working with bright students. Fortunately, there is ample opportunity for this at Governors State University near Chicago, where Jon is a member of the graduate faculty. Governors State, like most institutions of higher education, requires the faculty to publish in order to maintain academic excellence, stay current in the field, and create visibility and credibility for the university. So because Jon loves to teach, he complies with the expectation of publishing. Publishing enables him to use his talent for what he loves most: teaching.

Pat's story about publishing is a little more convoluted. It begins with the day she first meditated. While visiting a friend in San Francisco who had to work all day, Pat was left alone as a guest in the house. This was ideal, because being a guest meant that there was no temptation to do household chores, and this day occurred many years ago, before people had started carrying their work with them everywhere they went. There were no cell phones and no laptops, and this friend had no TV. So without planning or foresight, Pat meditated.

For a full day she sat still and was simply mindful of her thinking. She spent the day doing what she now knows as mindful meditation. At the time, all she did was take the time to complete every thought and pay attention. She concentrated on one thought at a time and gave it merit, regardless of the content. She sat quietly and let her mind do the work. During this day, many of the ideas that had been left incomplete by a busy life or a lack of focus had their chance to be heard, seen, and brought to a conclusion.

She thought about her life in general, her relationships, her future, and even her past, but ultimately the thoughts took shape around her work and the direction it should take. As she followed the mental trails and just watched her thinking progress, the direction kept leading to *First you've got to write a book*. Every path related to her career and to utilizing her talents led to this thought. Thus writing became a means to an end, a way to put her talent for learning and her desire to help others into meaningful action.

You may or may not be fully aware of your talents. If you aren't aware, it may be quite beneficial for you to take a talent retreat of sorts. Block off time when you are alone to just be mindful of your talents, your work, and how these relate to your core values, your connections, and a meaningful life.

Jhampa is a good example of someone who uses his numerous talents in meaningful ways. He makes his living as a Buddhist astrologer and a lay Buddhist teacher—these are obvious talents. He also has a talent for attention to detail, which makes him a fine tour guide, especially for the complexity of traveling in India. Leading groups to India is his way of using his gift of organization to benefit others and enable him to keep returning to his spiritual homeland.

When you travel with Jhampa, his thoughtful attention to detail is apparent. Security and constant vigilance seem to be paramount in his mind, and he goes to great lengths to make sure that you arrive safely at your destination with all your possessions intact. This is a tall order in India, because everywhere you go there are crowds of people. India is much smaller than the United States, but it has more than a billion people, so you can imagine the chaos that can occur just trying to get from a train station to a taxi. What seems like a swarm of humans comes at you, and they all want your business. (No wonder Jhampa sent a bunch of monks to pick us up at the airport.)

When our group finally gathered in Delhi to begin our trek to Dharamsala, Jhampa went into overdrive. He cautioned us, drilled us, and taught us the rules of the road ("Wear your backpacks in front when you are in a crowd")—all to ensure our safety. He had us surrounded by his Tibetan friends. We felt like the president with Secret Service agents or a Tour de France leader surrounded by his team. By the time we boarded the train to ride overnight from New Delhi to Punjab, we were not only inspired but informed. Thanks to Jhampa, we arrived intact and very grateful for the change of pace from the masses of the city to the majesty of the mountains.

The lodging that Jhampa had booked for us was in McLeod Ganj, a village inside the municipality of Dharamsala. He chose the Pema Thang Guest House, a quiet and peaceful hotel situated at the very end

of a street, tucked away from traffic, shops, and restaurants. Best of
all, every room had a balcony from which you could see the home and
headquarters of the Dalai Lama.

We'd traveled from North America, arrived in New Delhi, ridden
on a train for twelve hours and in a taxi for four hours, checked into the
hotel, and finally made it to our rooms in this magical place within
walking distance of the Dalai Lama. Everyone in our group did the
same thing. We all walked into our assigned rooms, opened the windows to reveal the glorious view, and then headed for the balconies to
look at Dharamsala. There we were, breathing in the mountain air, letting the weariness of travel wash away in the quiet of the mountains,
when suddenly we heard Jhampa's frantic voice screaming, "No-o-o-
o!" at us. We were startled out of our reveries as he came running into
the rooms. "Shut the windows! Shut the door!" he cried. "The monkeys
will get in and steal everything! They're mean; don't mess with them!"

We later found out Jhampa was right. The monkeys were quite
clever as well as aggressive. They would steal anything they could get
their hands on. But thanks to his ever-watchful eye and his voice of
experience, we all escaped the monkeyshines.

Jhampa takes great pride in sharing India with others in safety with
a pleasant manner. His fees for these excursions are only a small percentage of the fees charged by other vendors. Jhampa's tours are a labor
of love. They are an outlet for him to share with other Westerners what
he discovered in India. He finds deep meaning and takes great pride
in seeing others, like us, become changed through his facilitation of a
real-life encounter group. The passing on of what he has learned
becomes his way of saying thank you for all that he discovered through
his contacts with the Dalai Lama and other Buddhist teachers. Jhampa
uses his talents in meaningful ways.

Exercise 18: Discovering Your Talents

If it's been a while since you've taken stock of your talents or you've never surveyed them at all, we want to invite you to do this right now. Take as much time as you need to take a meaningful look at yourself.

Take in several deep breaths until you feel relaxed. When you are ready, close your eyes and imagine that you are talking with your mother. Ask her what she believes are your greatest strengths and talents. Breathe slowly and deeply as her ideas about your strengths appear. Avoid judging; just listen and let the thoughts fall like snowflakes. Now imagine that you are with your father and repeat the process. Do this with your grandparents, teachers, colleagues, siblings, children, friends, and partner until the ground is covered with the snowflakes of your talents and strengths. Notice as you breathe and pay attention.

When you are finished, write down the words or talents that come to mind or that stand out. This will help you to become more aware of your strengths.

When Your Work Lacks Meaning

When we meet someone for the first time, we usually ask, "What do you do?" Too many answers today reveal that people are out of work or believe that their work lacks meaning. A recent Gallup poll reports that only 20 percent of people in this country can give a strong "yes" to the question "Do you like what you do each day?" Many people are afraid, because they don't know where to go or what to do to find the connection that comes with meaningful work.

It's not surprising to find so few workers who like what they do each day, because so many jobs are built on shifting sands. According to psychologist and vocational counselor Mark Savickas, finding meaning, satisfaction, and connection through work becomes even more complex as organizations change shape. Projects replace jobs, and there is a frequent dislocation from the employment assignments that give meaning and significance to life. Uncertainty and insecurity rise because of recurrent transitions between assignments.

This "dejobbing" changes people from permanent employees to workers who are referred to as temporary, contingent, casual, contract, freelance, part-time, external, atypical, adjunct, consulting, and self-employed. Although some people prefer the flexibility and personal freedom that is inherent in this kind of work, many do not. There are drawbacks. Working this way does not provide the benefits of a traditional job: financial security, health insurance, the possibility of home ownership, and a pension. Such job changes can lead to loneliness and disconnection if one continues to see the world of work as it has been rather than as it has become.

"When I was in my midthirties," Jon states, "I was out of work and searched far and wide for employment to support my young children. Those days felt so empty, and I remember thinking that I was alone and inadequate in spite of the support I received from Laura, my family, and my friends. I felt dejected and rejected. I thought that no one really wanted me, that maybe I didn't have any real talent or ability, and that being out of work was all my fault; if only I had (fill in the blank).

"I remember those unhappy times of no employment, but I also remember another time when I had well-paid employment. It involved completing a project for the public schools that had already been axed (along with my position) as impossible. I had to go to work each day and write manuals for a curriculum that I knew would never be read, let alone used. I couldn't wake up, I didn't want to leave the house, and I hated the thought of having to go to work. I found excuse after excuse for why I couldn't make it to the office.

"These were two of the loneliest times in my life," Jon concludes. "As a man, I have always felt hardwired to be a provider and to work hard (probably way too hard)."

Dr. Savickas believes that today's worker needs to concentrate on employability, adaptability, emotional intelligence, and lifelong learning. The idea of finding a job in one organization for a lifetime is becoming less and less possible. To avoid the loneliness of unemployment, it is important to find meaning in your work, even in a world of job change.

Jon chuckles as he reads Dr. Savickas. "Where were you thirty years ago when I really needed this information?" he asks rhetorically. "I had to learn the hard way. I could not find a secure job at a university because the programs in my area of specialty were being eliminated. I eventually found work as a self-employed psychologist and returned to graduate school to receive additional training as a psychotherapist and clinical psychologist to improve my employability and adaptability. Fortunately, I began to focus on meaning as well as earning."

Right Intention: Finding Deeper Meaning in Your Work

The Dalai Lama's teachings on the concept of right intention give clear directions for meaningful work. Right intention has three components: (1) turning away from the lure of desire, (2) moving toward goodwill and core values, and (3) alleviating actions that create a harmful outcome. Practicing right intention in relation to your work may mean turning away from work that appeals only to your desires and not your core values. For work to have meaning, it must support your core values—that is, exemplify the characteristics you stand for.

Meaningful work will also allow for time and energy to be devoted to relationships with your friends and your family as well as with the broader community. Meaningful work should in no way produce a harmful outcome for you or others. Some jobs benefit a few people to the great disadvantage of many others. The material reward may be great, but what toll does it take on your soul? Right intention may mean turning away from the temptation of instant gratification through stuff. Stuff does not represent your core values but instead creates stress and guilt.

Finding deeper meaning in work has less to do with money than many people realize. Workers who believe that their talents are being recognized and utilized are, in general, happier with their pay scale.

Some of the most rewarding jobs and careers are not those with the highest pay. A *U.S. News & World Report* survey revealed that firefighters, locksmiths, clergy, landscape architects, and hairstylists all have high job satisfaction, and these jobs are not known for their high salaries. Can you imagine a firefighter or a member of the clergy saying, "Yeah, I'm in this for the money"?

Even if you'd like more money and don't have your dream job, your work can be meaningful if you recognize the connection between earning money and caring for people you love; this certainly fits the category of utilizing your talents in meaningful work. Millions of people go to work each day because they value providing for the people they love or simply being a productive member of society. They are grateful for the opportunity to be part of the workforce that sustains the social structure and supports everyday life. For your work to be more gratifying, you may need to trade money for meaning.

Another way to make work more meaningful is to work with people you like. If you have even one close friend at work, you'll be happier. Social contact is a human need and some of this needs to happen at work. Employers are recognizing this need for social contact, and many are sponsoring team-building activities and off-site recreational activities to strengthen the social network of the work community. People who like one another and get along are more productive. If you are among the 24 percent of Americans who work from home part-time or full-time, it might be more challenging to meet your needs for contact. If you are a homemaker or a full-time parent, you need contact with peers (other adults) who can supply support and social exchange in addition to your contact with the children. It is another way to make your work more meaningful.

Investing time and energy in your work community can improve its level of meaning for you. One group of women at an electronics factory collected money to paint and redecorate the women's lounge. They had such a great time on this project that they took their skills outside the plant and cleaned up the neighborhood playground. Investing adds meaning. Numerous work sites sponsor sports teams, social gatherings, philanthropic projects, and family gatherings. Taking time to participate in these activities can add meaning to your work through the connections and the support that you gain.

Thubten, who managed the restaurant at the Pema Thang Guest House, where we stayed in McLeod Ganj, had his own way of adding meaning to his work. One meal was all it took to convince us that this was no ordinary restaurant. Thubten prepared each dish from scratch, and when it was gone, that was it. So, for example, if you wanted the tasty muesli he prepared every morning, you had to get there early to get your share.

Thubten was a master at doing one thing at a time, and there was no interrupting him. When he cooked, he cooked; when he cleaned, he cleaned. The restaurant was spotless. His presence gave it a sacred feeling. We felt this when we met him and even more after one morning when we arrived early for breakfast and found the lights off and no customers present. Thubten sat on a cushion near a window, chanting and saying prayers in front of a makeshift altar that he kept hidden behind the curtains. We knew that our intuition had been correct: the restaurant was literally and figuratively his temple.

Thubten had found many ways to make his work meaningful. Now we want to provide you with an opportunity to assess how meaningful your work is.

Exercise 19: **Is My Work Meaningful?**

Rate each statement accordingly:

1 = Strongly Agree   **4** = Disagree
2 = Agree   **5** = Strongly Disagree
3 = Neither or not applicable

_____ 1. My work is rewarding.

_____ 2. My work is in an intriguing or energizing field.

_____ 3. My work allows me to express or live by certain standards, principles, or values.

_____ 4. My work allows me to give back, share, change, or improve something that makes a difference either internally or externally.

_____ 5. My work lets me solve problems or answer complex questions in some way.

_____ 6. My work changes, modifies, or alters my lifestyle, priorities, or relationships in a positive manner.

_____ 7. My work is something I feel passionate about.

_____ 8. My work supports an important cause.

_____ 9. My work lets me innovate or create something new or original.

_____ 10. My work enables me to gain knowledge, understanding, or expertise through experience or study.

_____ 11. My work allows ample time for me to maintain connections to friends and family.

_____ 12. My work is congruent with my core values.

How did you score?

50–60 Looks like a great job.

30–49 Could use some improvement.

15–29 Meaning is low.

14 and below Time for a change?

Which areas are absent in your current position? Which ones are most pleasing? Most disappointing? Can you think of ways to change your score and keep your job? Can you think of a different job that might allow you to attain a more satisfying score?

Changing your job may be the most efficient way to give meaning to your work, but in today's climate that can be difficult. You can also increase your happiness simply by changing your view of your job or career, without changing where you work. Here are some examples of how to do this:

- You can recognize the greater good that results from your work. A person's routine responsibilities in a fitness center can take on greater meaning by recognizing the center's role in promoting health and wellness in the community. A police officer might take pride in a neighborhood's increased safety.

- You can focus on the importance of your role in the larger organization. Someone who is responsible for maintaining a school can keep in mind that a well-maintained building teaches the students to have pride in whatever they do.

- You can focus more on the relationships that are part of your work. A teacher who is grading papers can see this feedback as an important way to let the students know that they are valued and that their papers have been carefully read.

When you change your attitude toward right intention, you change the meaning in your work, your relationships, and your life.

Golden Handcuffs

Some of you may fall into the I-hate-my-job-but-I-love-the-money category; if you relate to this, be careful. Make sure that you are not trading your time and energy simply to provide more of the stuff that clutters your life and sacrifices well-being. If you are working to provide your children with an excess of goods and services that turn them into demanding, easily bored, insatiable creatures who believe that the word *delayed* applies only to a rained-out ballgame and who think that gratification is their inalienable right, then you are raising children who will grow up to continue the cycle of loneliness.

If you are bound by golden handcuffs, check out your reference group—that is, the people with whom you compare yourself and the standards by which you evaluate your lifestyle. Television has drastically changed our lifestyle expectations. Because TV reaches such a broad spectrum of people and because about the same percentage of millionaires and billionaires watch TV as those with less income, the focus is aimed at those with the most money, because they have more to spend on the products advertised by the sponsors.

Unfortunately, the rest of us are also watching, and somehow we think that we, too, should have a kitchen that is twenty feet by thirty feet, a closetful of designer clothes, a vast array of technological gadgets, and an SUV to take on vacation every year. This looks like standard fare in the United States. But as Boston College sociologist Juliet B. Schor wrote in *The Overspent American*, to come close to the average lifestyle we see on television—not even the rich and famous genre, but just everyday TV—you'd need a minimum of $250,000 per year!

Far too many people are living a lifestyle way beyond their means. Most are caught in a vicious cycle of work and spend: working long, hard hours at their jobs, then feeling justified in spending money to reward themselves with the stuff of instant gratification. However, the more you spend, the more pressure there is to work—whether the work is meaningful or not. You have to keep on working at a job you don't like to pay for what you don't even enjoy that much. The more stuff you have, the less pleasure it gives you.

One study asked a group of people, "Which would you rather have: an income of $50,000 and everyone else gets $25,000 or an income of $100,000 and everyone else gets $200,000?" Most chose half as much money, $50,000, just to have more than everyone else. They could have chosen twice the amount for themselves, but it was more important to them to have more money than others instead of just more money for themselves.

If you are attached to the lifestyles portrayed in the media, if you are determined to have twice as much as your neighbor, or if you are letting someone else dictate your happiness and satisfaction based on selling *their* products and *their* standards, you will be caught in a trap that will never use your talents in a meaningful way. The cost of this luxury may be loneliness. You can break the golden handcuffs with core value living.

Core Value Living

If your talents are not being utilized in meaningful work, but you feel locked into the golden handcuffs created by money, you might need to take a mindful look at changing your life. You might choose to live a lifestyle that is simpler. Some call this living beneath your means; however, it might be more accurate to call it living within your means, or core value living.

The economic challenges we are living with today have inspired many people to do just this. The *New York Times* recently featured a couple who was inspired by the 100 Thing Challenge, a pledge to cull your belongings to a mere 100 items. These two people began to right-size their lives by donating extra clothes to charity, but as the months went by, they started to shed books, pots and pans, and ultimately their cars. They now reside in a 400-square-foot apartment in Portland, Oregon. He is completing a doctorate, and she works from home. They are still car-free and have bikes.

One thing they don't have is debt. When you live simply and are not encumbered by debt, you are not bound by golden handcuffs. You can choose your work based on the meaningful use of your talents, or you can take a job to pay the bills and have time to dedicate to meaningful activities such as volunteer work, hobbies, or projects—all of which prevent loneliness and create happiness.

Core value living creates a lifestyle of safety, calm, and flexibility. You won't be locked into meaningless work if you live beneath your means and save money. A financial safety net can enable you to make a transition in work, if that is necessary in the future. Living beneath your means doesn't mean you will be deprived. If you are letting your core values guide your spending, you might (like the couple we just mentioned) have the best bicycle money can buy but no car or an older used car. If you are letting your core values guide your spending, you might live in a small home but have money for travel and adventure.

Core value living is guided by right intention; this means that your choices are in line with who you are and who you want to be. Right intention also means that your choices do not create a harmful outcome for you or for others.

Exercise 20: **Core Value Living**

We are going to ask you to do this meditation exercise in bed right before you fall asleep. Prepare for bed as usual; lie in a comfortable position, preferably on your back with your eyes closed. You may need a pillow for support under your knees. Relax; take three deep breaths, and begin to imagine what your life would look like with core value living.

Imagine where you would live. See the place clearly and notice how large or small it is; look around at the furnishings and change anything that would have to be changed to fall in line with core value living. Once you get a picture of where you would live, take a deep breath and feel what it is like to be there. Hear the sounds or the silence of this place; taste the taste and smell the smells. Pay attention to your body in this place.

Now shift your focus to core value living at work. Imagine where you would work. See the place clearly and notice how large or small it is; see the activity in this place and change anything that would have to be changed to fall in line with core value living at work. Once you get a picture of this workplace, take a deep breath and feel what it is like to be there. Hear the sounds or the silence of this place; taste the taste and smell the smells. Pay attention to your body in this place.

Finally, shift your focus to core value living at leisure. Imagine a place where you might enjoy your leisure time. Once you imagine a place, take your core value leisure time to another place. Find a place you really enjoy and take a moment to look around more thoroughly. See the place of leisure clearly and notice what's happening; see who is there with you. Hear the sounds of this place; taste the taste, smell the smells, and feel what it is like to be at leisure in core value living.

Finish this exercise by letting your thoughts travel where they will, then let yourself fall sleep. Pay attention in the morning to any dreams you've had. Feel yourself move toward core value living.

Overdoing It

The last culprit in the connection between loneliness and work is overdoing it. Even meaningful work that utilizes your talents and supports your core values can lead to loneliness if it takes too much time from the other important connections in your life.

Because work can serve so many important functions in our lives, it is easy to overdo it. Through meaningful work we get the pleasure of accomplishment, the opportunity to help others, and the joy of collaboration. Work often provides a source of social support and community; some of the finest friendships are formed at work, and many people even meet their future mates at work. Certainly the money we earn from work puts food on the table and clothes in our closets. But because the reward system of work is multifaceted, it can lure us into a state of stimulation that makes other activities pale by comparison. Work can fill your time and your world, especially if you don't know who you are, aren't skilled at connecting to others, and are not involved or invested in community activities. Even if you have friends and family waiting for you at home, if you invest only in work, home life can seem dull or tedious by comparison.

Current technology has fueled the allure of work by enabling us to be connected 24/7. We can access e-mails, close deals, get necessary information, share jokes with coworkers, finish conversations, and be expected to be available by phone at any time of the day or night, regardless of where we are. Because we spend so much time at work and, for many of us, work is interesting, conversation flows freely between coworkers; there's always something to talk about. Friendships and bonds are formed because your time and your energy are focused on the same goals when you work together.

If you are not careful to keep work in balance with life outside work, the time and the energy you invest will make work more appealing than your life at home and the people in it. Because you can stay connected even when you are not at the workplace, you can take coworkers as well as projects home with you. In essence, your body may be home, but your mind can still be at work. Because of the stimulating nature of technology and the ease of accessibility, millions of people are sliding

into a state of overwork that seems quite normal. But there is ultimately a cost, and the price may include loneliness.

Are You Overdoing It?

You know you are overdoing it when you work when you don't have
to, when you are more attached to the people at work than the people
at home, when you text and tweet and go on Facebook and fantasize
about people who don't live with you, or when it is more exciting to
check your work e-mail than to check in face-to-face with friends or
family. This may sound confusing; how is this loneliness?

Go back and check your core values. Is this how you want to be
remembered by the people you love? Is this how you stay connected to
close friends and family? Is this how you invest in the community?
Overdoing it at work takes energy that rightfully belongs to your
friends, family, community, and overall purpose in life. There are five
major causes of loneliness (the topics of Chapters 3–7), and when you
are tending only to the cause related to work, you are ignoring the
other four causes. When you invest an inordinate amount of time,
energy, and interest in work you become more and more disconnected
from yourself, from your home, from your community, and from your
overall purpose in life, and loneliness will ultimately follow. The
meaning you get from work will not alleviate the other four causes of
loneliness.

You know you are overdoing it when work takes a toll on your
health. Some people actually work themselves to death. In Japan,
karoshi, death by overwork, is estimated to cause one thousand deaths
per year. In the Netherlands, overwork has resulted in a new condition
known as "leisure illness"; workers actually get physically sick on week-
ends and vacations as they try to relax.

In the United States, leisure illness isn't a problem for most people
because thousands of vacation days are not even taken. Workers feel
too anxious about leaving work to take time off; they fear reprisal from

their superiors, or they suffer from guilt that they will be letting their coworkers down if they take off the time they have earned. Some fear that if they take leave, the company will discover that it can function without them and eliminate their jobs. Others are more honest: they'd just rather be at work than at home or on vacation.

You know you are overdoing it when people you love complain—or just plain miss you. When you are behind on many of your important relationships, when you don't get together with people and just hang out, when you have to make an appointment weeks or months in advance to see close friends or family members, or when you've shifted your social life from home to work, you know you are overdoing it.

Only you know what to do if you are overdoing it. Better people than us have probably tried to get you to curtail the time and energy you spend at work. So we are going to ask you directly and simply to address the issue in the next exercise.

Exercise 21: **Undoing Overdoing**

This exercise is short and sweet. If you answer no to the first question, skip the rest.

1. Are you overdoing work?
2. If so, how?
3. What do you need to do about it?
4. What's the first step?
5. When will you take it?

Right Livelihood

If you study the great teachers of Buddhism, from any of its tradition, you will find that they pretty much agree on what right livelihood is not. They will tell you that dealing in weapons, slavery, prostitution, poisons, or intoxicants is wrong livelihood. In essence, they all say, anything that is dishonest or harmful to others is wrong livelihood. This obviously creates a great contradiction in the context of modern culture. Many of the jobs or careers we admire and aspire toward actually require deceit, hypocrisy, treachery, and trickery. I am sure that we all could come up with examples to illustrate that.

If you have been at all aware since 2008, you can't have missed the economic tsunami that was created by a few companies and individuals who didn't care about the impact of their work on the global community. Many of us are still recovering from the devastating effects of selfish practices that gave little or no regard to others. The Buddha's concept of right, or effective, livelihood has very little to do with accumulating money and everything to do with whether your choices contribute to the overall happiness of the world. It is more about internal values than external rewards. With this frame of reference, we ask the following questions:

What is the nature of your work—and how does it affect your nature?

What are the ethical standards of this work?

How does your work relate to the greater good of your community (and the world), and how does it affect you?

Most of us have to work for a living. Do you just think about the money it affords?

Money buys happiness. (At least, some money buys some happiness, according to psychologist Dan Gilbert.) What is the cost to you and others of the money your work provides?

All spiritual traditions teach the importance of making a contribution and doing your part to earn a living and sustain yourself, but we are taking it one step further. We are talking about not only supporting yourself but also working in a manner that does no harm and then has meaning. Our daily lives are balanced by the ebb and flow of activity and inactivity, creativity and contemplation. Work helps us to structure our lives in a productive manner. Work makes rest sweeter. If all you ever do is rest, it will no longer be restful. The key is balance. How balanced is your life and your work?

If work is contributing to your loneliness, determine whether this is because the work doesn't use your talents, lacks meaning, involves golden handcuffs, or involves overworking. Reread the sections on these topics and use the suggestions to never be lonely again.

Whatever your talents and abilities may be, using these gifts in a meaningful way can connect you to your core values and connect you to others: friends, family members, or strangers. Using your talents in a meaningful way can be a small act of kindness or consciousness, like picking up items off the floor of a department store, sharing vegetables from your garden with a neighbor, or (in Jhampa's case) sharing your friend the Dalai Lama with others. When you use your particular talent in a meaningful way, you make a connection that has no space for loneliness.

7

Am I Living Out the Purpose of My Life?

THE PURPOSE IN LIFE IS A
LIFE OF PURPOSE.

—Robert Byrne, author

I f we asked you to list three words or phrases that describe Mother
Teresa, what would you choose? Would *kind, compassionate,* or *caring* come to mind? Or would you think of *Nobel Peace Prize winner
or world-class humanitarian*? Our hunch is that of all the descriptors you
might choose, the word lonely would not be among them—not just
because she was most often depicted in the midst of a crowd, but
because she exuded anything but loneliness.

That's because her life had purpose. She was a woman on a mission,
and she wasn't shy about chastising others for wasting her time. On
numerous occasions she told reporters to "quit wasting time with questions and go feed the poor." One of her more well-known challenges
was "If you can't feed a hundred people, then feed just one!" Feeding
the poor, ministering to the sick, and housing the orphaned were part
of her purpose. You might say that she was too busy to be lonely, but
busyness doesn't prevent loneliness; you have to have purpose. Without
purpose, part of you is missing, and this missing part creates a loneliness that can be filled only by having an important reason to live.

Having a purpose connects you to life itself. We were reminded of this fact during an interview with a woman named Lillian who had struggled with loneliness. Despite having friends and family members who loved her and a career that she loved for twenty years, Lillian felt extremely lonely and desperate to find a purpose for her life. During difficult times, she felt guilty that she wasn't more grateful, and she was perplexed that her work did not hold the passion it once had. Her relationships and her career had always given her a sense of purpose, but now they did not. Lillian's life lacked purpose, and the situation was painful.

Then, seemingly by accident and much to her surprise, Lillian discovered that she had a talent for glassblowing, of all things. It was love at first sight. With her newly acquired skill, Lillian created vases, bowls, dishes, glass jewelry, and works of art. She sold her skill, taught it, and gave it away. Passionate about her avocation, Lillian once again felt a sense of purpose in her life.

In another interview we met Don, who found purpose by providing Driving Miss Daisy, a taxi service of sorts for older women who were no longer able to drive. He told us that Driving Miss Daisy gave him more pleasure than his former career as an engineer ever had. His new-found purpose also alleviated the loneliness he had been feeling since his wife died.

It was a pleasure to meet Don as well as Lillian; both were full of life.

A person with purpose, whether it is Mother Teresa or a man with a taxi service, is an energy magnet. We love being around people with purpose, because they motivate, challenge, energize, and attract us. People with purpose are not lonely, because others are drawn to them. When Mother Teresa died, her Missionaries of Charity had 610 missions in 123 countries. Her work continues because of the dedication of those who share her passion and her purpose.

You may know someone who would be happy to share his or her passion with you, whether it is for glassblowing, baking, or bicycle repair.

If you are unclear about your purpose, there's no harm in sharing someone else's for a while. You can borrow his or hers until you either adopt it as your own or discover another one for yourself.

Knowing your purpose offsets loneliness in two ways, one external and one internal. Discovering your purpose puts you in touch with a unique source of energy similar to synergy; it's the energy you feel when you connect with someone around a task or an interest, and the result is greater than the sum of both your efforts. When you tap into a purposeful activity, you connect with a power source; you become energized, and others recognize the life force in you. This is the external effect.

Life energy, also known as libido, is attractive and engaging. Your energy will be contagious, and others will want to catch it. People will notice and be drawn to you; this is simply a natural by-product of being purposeful about life. In addition, most people find that a life purpose includes meaningful contact with other people, whether it's sharing their talents with admirers or teaching soccer to seven-year-olds.

In terms of an internal effect, discovering what you are on Earth for gives you a sense of calm and confidence. No longer will you feel anxious or uncertain about the reason for your existence or the direction of your life. This contentment will have a positive effect on your contact with each person you encounter. In addition, having a purpose takes away the need to cling or be dependent on other people for your passion or your power. Purposeful living will make you feel connected to life itself and take away the fifth cause of loneliness.

You don't have to search far to discover the connection between feeling lonely and lacking a purpose in life. Our interviews with people who were struggling with loneliness revealed the connection immediately. Time and again we heard some version of "I'm not sure why I'm here" or "I don't have any goals or purpose." There were also variations such as "I don't feel useful" or "My life doesn't have meaning." We were struck by the frequency of these comments and the wealth of research that links a lack of purpose to loneliness.

Stephen Covey, in his bestselling book *The 7 Habits of Highly Effective People*, reiterates the importance of having clear mental vision and purpose. A great deal of his work is based on the fact that people who are mentally healthy and happy commit themselves to the values, principles, and purposes that they establish. He found in his research that being aware of your life purpose starts a process of regular self-assessment and self-correction that enables you to stay on course with your life. Success comes to people who make a goal and follow the course to that goal.

Your life purpose, whether or not you are aware of it, guides the decisions you make. Even a belief that you have no life purpose will have an influence. Your purpose in life provides the broad guidelines you follow as you make plans for the future. When you are living out your purpose, your days are more organized, content, and energized; rarely will loneliness be part of that experience.

Having a life purpose is very practical. If at any time you become overwhelmed or stressed by life's demands, or even just bored or cranky with a day's activities, you can stop and ask yourself "What is my purpose in life?" and get back on track. Do a small thing that fits into your life purpose, and contentment will be restored. It's such a worthy goal to determine your life purpose, and it's more harmful than you might realize to be living a life without purpose. An elementary understanding of the concept of anomie will explain why.

Anomie

Anomie is the feeling of anxiety that comes from having no direction, goal, or purpose. This aimlessness occurs when you lack an internal compass to guide you through life. At the end of the eighteenth century, French sociologist Émile Durkheim popularized the term when he used it to explain the malaise and despondency that can lead to suicide. In his book *Suicide*, Durkheim described how fatalistic thoughts arise when one has no purpose or legitimate aspirations. If you feel this anxiety or despondency, we suggest that you let it serve as a catalyst to motivate you to stay on the path of discovery. You have complete control over these feelings; let them guide you to your purpose in life.

If you are seeking your purpose in life, you are not alone. This fact was reinforced when *The Purpose Driven Life* by Rick Warren became a bestseller. To date, this book has sold more copies than any other book in U.S. history. In the first five years of publication, more than 30 million copies were sold, and it stayed on the *New York Times* Best Sellers list for one of the longest periods in U.S. history.

On the cover of *The Purpose Driven Life* is the question "What on earth am I here for?" Apparently there are many people who are searching for the answer, and it makes sense. Knowing your purpose on Earth provides a rationale for your existence. It gives direction, focus, and meaning to life. Without purpose, how will you decide which decisions are right for you? How will you direct your life? How will you measure your progress? Without purpose, you will long for what can easily be the most important part of yourself—the part that makes your existence relevant and provides personal fulfillment.

How do you proceed to find your life purpose? In his book, Reverend Warren states that your purpose in life can be found only through understanding and doing what God placed you on Earth to do. This point of view will undoubtedly make sense to many of you, but for others it may not. Examining your life's purpose naturally brings up religious, spiritual, and perhaps philosophical questions that we are not going to try to answer for you. Instead, we will provide guidelines and suggestions to use as you answer the questions for yourself. Discovering your purpose is a personal process, and it is well worth the time and effort.

Finding and Clarifying Your Purpose

We have organized this book in a manner designed to lead you to your purpose in life, or at least to move you in the right direction. Answering the first four questions—Who am I? Am I connected? Am

I in community? Are my talents utilized in meaningful work?—can certainly increase the quality of everyday life. If you practice making your thoughts and your actions exemplify your core values, if you honor and invest in the people to whom you are connected, if you devote time to making your community a better place, and if your talents are utilized in meaningful work, the chances are that you already believe that your life has purpose. Some of you may want to go a step further. Let's look at some ways to do this.

Acknowledge What Is

Sara Beth, one of the people who are reading this book and providing feedback as we write it says that defining her purpose has been extremely helpful at this time in her life.

"During the past several months," she says, "it seems like every friend I have is in crisis. Hardly a day goes by that I don't get a distress call from someone I love who has a serious issue going on. Right now I have a friend whose husband just had a heart attack; another friend whose son lost his job, and he has to support three children; another whose husband is bedridden, and her health is also very bad; a couple who has two daughters, both on drugs; a relative whose daughter and son-in-law got put in jail for child endangerment when stopped for driving under the influence of drugs; and a friend whose business is failing and taking her life savings down with it.

"I could go on. When these calls started coming at a rate of two or three a day, at first I felt guilty for taking so much time away from work and my other commitments; but then I realized, *This is my purpose in life; supporting friends in need is the gift I can offer to those who have been so wonderful to me over the course of my life.* When I recognized and acknowledged the importance of this activity, my attitude changed, and I felt energized by the opportunity."

You may already know your purpose in life, but perhaps have not recognized it as such. We suggest that you be more intentional about it; you might be surprised and delighted at the direction and energy it provides for you once you make the acknowledgment.

Think Like a Child

More than once we've heard people of a mature age laughingly say, "I don't know what I want to be when I grow up." As odd as it might sound, to find out what is important to you, to find your purpose in life, you might start by looking at what you enjoyed doing as a child. One track of career theory states that your interests and talents are most evident at a young age; therefore, if you look back at the activities that got your attention or were important to you throughout childhood and adolescence, you might discover a link to your life purpose.

Some people know their purpose in life fairly early. We have a friend who was called to the ministry at age ten and never looked back. He's still an active pastor at age seventy. For most of us, the direction isn't quite as clear, or if it was clear, we got derailed somewhere along the way.

Pat is a classic example of someone who got derailed. "When I was in third grade," she recalls, "I wrote a play. It wasn't an assignment or part of the schoolwork; I just got an idea to write a script for a play for the class to perform. It was fun, and I enjoyed the writing. In middle school, essay questions were my favorite; I loved exploring thoughts on paper. Later, in high school, I had an English teacher, Haymond Plaugher, who was an incredible inspiration to my writing. He made composition fun. When I was seventeen, I recall a conversation with my father asking me about my plans for the future. I said, 'I'd like to be a journalist.'

"I loved writing and research, but my mother wanted me to be a nurse. She had wanted this career for herself but had never achieved it, and she thought it might be a fine career path for me. So, following my mother's wishes, I enrolled in a four-year degree program in nursing. Big mistake; I hated it. I was depressed, I gained thirty pounds in one year, and I went from being a high school honor student to being on the edge of academic probation in college.

"Even an English composition course I was required to take became an additional disappointment when the professor basically told me I couldn't write. In fact, she used a poem I wrote as an example of bad writing for the class after us. I discovered that she used the poem accidentally, and the humiliation buried my interest in writing for almost twenty years. I was a miserable failure and became a college dropout.

"Years later I returned to complete a bachelor's degree and then a master's; when I got to my doctoral studies and was faced with writing a dissertation, I was overwhelmed. But I was fortunate enough to have a major professor, Dr. Sherry Cormier, who guided me through the process with her simple instruction 'Just give me something to correct.' She took the pressure off and helped to restore my confidence and commitment to writing. Even though I got derailed for several years," Pat concludes, "I ultimately found my way back to a purposeful life, and writing is an important part of that purpose."

Looking at your history might give you some interesting information about your purpose in life. We ask you to think back: What types of activities did you enjoy as a child? Did you ever declare an interest in a profession or an activity? What types of games did you play? What were your interests in school? What jobs or professions seemed interesting to you? What seemed attractive about growing up?

If any of the questions pique your curiosity, we suggest that you find a quiet place and set aside time to contemplate and meditate. You may recall the story about the day that Pat first practiced mindfulness—the first time she sat still for an entire day without talking and just took time to focus on her thoughts about her life. The stillness of the day, as well as the opportunity to finish each thought, provided a powerful experience that later revealed a more purposeful path.

Here's how Jon answered some of the questions from childhood. "As a kid I had many interests and was involved in a wide range of activities.

I couldn't wait for school to end so I could play with the many friends in the neighborhood. I looked forward to games but really never liked sitting inside practicing piano or other musical instruments. I was often the organizer of the activities and never seemed to have problems finding people to play with. I enjoyed humor and getting into mischief. I mowed several neighbors' lawns and shoveled their snow until I was old enough to get a real job."

By addressing the questions we have posed to you, Jon detected some patterns that led to his life today, especially the connections with his peers and community. He admits that it was very hard for him to figure out his life purpose. Maybe others could see it, but not Jon. In college he couldn't choose a major; business seemed too dog-eat-dog, law didn't seem honorable, and math and science were not much fun. So by default he became an education major. Because he didn't know what he wanted to teach, he ended up in elementary school, where you have to teach everything. This suited him fine.

In high school he had known most of the almost two thousand kids as well as the teachers. He was not the best student but was popular, athletic, and elected to leadership positions. He always seemed to be up for hanging out with whoever wanted to hang out. He played basketball, swam, went to the pool hall, and hung out on the corner or wherever the kids were congregating. In hindsight he realizes just how people-oriented he was and how strong his longing to help people was. Once this was understood, he excelled. He was so energized that he went on to earn degrees in elementary education, guidance counseling, psychotherapy, and clinical psychology. He earned not one doctoral degree but two! Once he found his purpose, he loved it and knew it was the right fit.

Can you see any connection between your early interests and a direction for your life now? Are there any messages that you have ignored? Have you gotten derailed or are you on track? What would it take to get you back on track? Are you living out the purpose of your life? If not, what step should you take next to move you in the right direction?

Follow the Energy

Earlier we mentioned that people who are living a life of purpose are like energy magnets. They attract others and bond easily around a mutual interest. Libido, or life energy, is so contagious. When you are following your purpose in life, you are energized. It takes little effort to get excited, be absorbed in a task, stay focused, and even lose track of time. Take a close look at what excites you, what gives you energy. Following your purpose in life should be an energizing experience.

How do you spend your free time? What activity inspires you? What do you anticipate that also makes you feel good about yourself? What do you do easily that improves the lives of others? What do people thank you for that seems to take hardly any effort at all or is even a pleasure for you? The answers to these questions may reflect your purpose in life. Remember that your purpose in life does not have to include being paid to do it.

If you are still unclear or want to further clarify your purpose, let us pose more questions to sharpen your awareness. What are your aspirations? What do you daydream about for the years ahead? Five years from now, what do you think you will wish you had done? What would you do if you knew you could not fail at it? What could you do that would make you proud of yourself? What could you do that would show that you were living a life in line with your core values?

Taking a different perspective, we ask the following: How do you fill your physical space? What objects are most important to you? What might someone who walked through your home say about you? What might he or she say is important to the person living there?

How do you spend your time? How much is for work? For fun? For maintenance? How much of your time are you alone? How much are you with other people? Are you comfortable with your friends?

How do you spend your energy? What things do you feel you must do each day? What are you never too tired to do? What excites you?

How do you spend your money? Would you be seen as frivolous, tight, or generous? Are you more of a saver or a spender?

In what area of life are you most organized? In what area are you least organized? Does this need to change?

When are you most self-disciplined? What activities do you do well, and which ones can you just barely get done? Do you like to be in groups, or do you prefer individual pursuits?

What do you think about? What do you visualize? What do you talk to yourself about? What do you talk to others about? How would your life be different if you had the education or training you desired?

What about you inspires others? What do you stand for? What is your attitude toward life? In what ways do you contribute to the community?

If you had one day to live, what would you do? What do you want your obituary to say about you?

What are your goals? Assume for a moment that your purpose in life is quite evident, but you just have to see it. What is the obvious answer to the question "What is your purpose in life?"

Jhampa's Journey to Purpose

When we were in India, we asked Jhampa to tell us how a Westerner ended up in the Indian Himalayas speaking several new languages and practicing a totally different way of life. Here's part of his story (reprinted with permission from Jeffrey Kottler and Jon Carlson's *Moved by the Spirit*):

Mark Shaneman's (later to become Jhampa) father died when he was six, leaving a huge hole in his life. In the years immediately after his father's death he simply walked through life following the steps through grade school and ultimately high school. But after his high school graduation he felt a restlessness that wouldn't let him go on to University. He knew he might go some day, but not right away. He was feeling discouraged and dispirited by the state of the world—including the war in Vietnam and a general sense of meaninglessness in his life. He wanted to take some time off and see the world. Thus far he had spent his childhood on a farm, and his teen years in Vancouver, British Columbia.

Mark found himself a good job, earning a solid wage, and enough to buy a brand-new car. He was supporting himself in his own apartment at a time when most of his friends still lived at home. He had money to spare to go to rock concerts and buy whatever he wanted. He partied a lot, entertained his friends, and generally had a pretty good life. Still, he was not particularly happy,

Whether as a sign of impulsiveness, desperation, or pure lust for adventure, Mark decided that it was time to venture out into the world. Like many young people during this era, he decided to see Europe and sold all his belongings to finance the expedition.

After several months traveling throughout the continent, he made his way across Turkey, Iran, Iraq, Afghanistan, and then down into India. For Mark, India was love at first sight. He became immediately intrigued with the rich culture, the temples every-where, the atmosphere steeped in spirituality. As an added bonus, they [the people] even spoke English, making things far more accessible than [in] the Middle East.

Mark's first reaction to India was that it felt to him like he was coming home. This puzzled him as he noted his reaction in his diary because India was so exotic, so for-eign, so different from his native Canada. He hadn't been looking for anything within the realm of the spiritual but he was nevertheless intrigued by the way of life. Every street corner had a temple. There were ringing bells and flowers everywhere, sym-bols of the devotion to religion. The people were incredibly welcoming and gracious.

In India he felt a huge weight being lifted off his shoulders, although at the time he couldn't explain what it was. All he knew is that he was tired of people back home asking him all the time what he was going to do with his life. He had no idea. Yet in India nobody had any expectations for him. For the first time in as long as he could remember he felt free.

A Bowl of Oatmeal

Eventually Mark ended up in central India, at a place where a number of spiri-tual teachers converged—mostly exiled Buddhist monks from Tibet who practiced the tradition of Mahayana Buddhism. Mark had thought it would be interesting to learn how to meditate—something of a rite of passage for a young man traveling in the East.

One of the first tenets of Buddhism is that your attitude is your creator; the mind is everything. For Mark, this was a major revelation. He took to the meditation right away and enjoyed the introductory sessions with his first teacher. When he heard that a well-known Tibetan *lama*, i.e., spiritual leader, was going to give a talk he immediately made plans to check it out.

There were seven or eight people crowded into a tiny room next to a *stupa*—a 2,000-year-old religious monument several hundred feet tall. The room couldn't have been more than five by seven feet with a single entrance where a round-faced monk was sitting on the floor. Mark's first thought was that the monk looked like the happiest person he'd ever seen. He had an amazing smile that seemed to fill all the available space in the room. All of Mark's previous experience with religious figures had been that they seemed dour and serious. This guy was quite a surprise.

"Within seconds," Mark recalled, "I understood that this guy really knew the mind, and I am not talking about some kind of psychic thing. This fellow, as he talked about Tibetan Buddhism, gave me the sense that there were so many interesting levels of the experience. It was like eating a bowl of oatmeal. It is really nice and nourishing. If you put a little butter on it, the oatmeal might be even more delicious. But this monk, Lama Yeshe, was like a three-course meal and every dish was a little different. It was just spectacular; more than I could hope to digest."

As Lama Yeshe continued to speak about the dharma (Buddhist teachings) and the Buddhist way, Mark felt himself come under a spell of sorts. It was as if he felt an explosion inside of him that changed everything in his life. By the time the talk was over Mark found himself wandering the streets, thinking about what had transpired in that little room and how different he felt. He was determined to seek out Lama Yeshe to become his student and learn more about Buddhism. Little did he realize that he would remain in India for the next fourteen years and become one of the first Westerners to ever become a Tibetan Buddhist monk.

From Mark to Jhampa

There were two things that came together for Mark Shaneman during his initial studies and initiation into the rites as a Buddhist monk. The first was realizing that the mind is the creator of both happiness and sadness. Second, and perhaps most important in the life of a twenty-year-old man without a father, was recognizing that becoming a monk was like joining an all-men's club. All of the monks with whom he studied were older, wise men who served not only as mentors and spiritual guides but also as father figures. It felt to Mark as if he truly had found his home.

Within six months of having begun his studies with Lama Yeshe, Mark journeyed to Katmandu, Nepal, in order to become ordained as a Buddhist monk. He not only changed the course of his life, but his whole identity—including his name, which became Jhampa.

Upon returning to India after the induction into the Tibetan spiritual tradition, Jhampa was scheduled to meet with His Holiness the Dalai Lama. At this time, in 1971, the Dalai Lama was only thirty-six years old, the same age as Lama Yeshe. His Holiness had, as yet, little contact with the West and almost no interactions with a Western initiate like Jhampa. There were not more than a handful of Western monks who had gone through the Tibetan system in the whole world.

Jhampa was nervous enough about an audience with the Dalai Lama but felt somewhat reassured that he would not have to do or say anything. He would merely be an observer to the proceedings between his teacher and His Holiness. When the day arrived, Lama Yeshe had an emergency to attend to and so could not keep his appointment, leaving Jhampa to fend for himself during the meeting.

Jhampa was twenty years old, newly ordained, living in a strange country, unable to speak the Tibetan language, and about to meet with one of the most revered spiritual leaders in the world. What in the world would he say to such a person who is regarded by some as a god?

Jhampa decided to prepare for the interview by reading a book about the essence of Buddhist philosophy that discussed how everything in the world is merely a reflection of your own mind. He had hoped that reviewing this material might give him an idea for a question he might pose to His Holiness when they met.

Jhampa showed up for the audience to find himself alone with the Dalai Lama and his private secretary, who would act as a translator. Jhampa looked the part as an apprentice monk, shaved head, and simple robe, but he felt way out of his league walking into a meeting like this. He was just a kid who felt like he was playing dress-up.

Jhampa knew enough to offer the traditional greeting of three prostrations (he had been practicing the reverentially prone position). He then seated himself on the floor, legs crossed underneath him, and waited patiently for a signal to begin. When the Dalai Lama nodded, Jhampa took a deep breath.

"If the world is a reflection of your mind," he framed his question to the Master, "then does the world have any reality to it whatsoever?" Waiting for the translation, and then seeing a blank look on His Holinesses' [sic] face, Jhampa continued in this vein for another five minutes of elaboration. He asked about the meaning of consciousness and the mind, the psychology of Buddhism, and more esoteric philosophy, yet the more he went on the more uncomfortable he started to feel. This was not going at all as he had anticipated.

A minute went by, or perhaps even longer (it surely felt longer), before the Dalai Lama spoke. When he did, Jhampa was taken aback that the words were in English: "Do you know when you are going to die?"

"Excuse me, Your Holiness?" Jhampa said, startled by this question. He couldn't quite wrap his mind around it. Had he heard correctly? He looked toward the translator for confirmation, but he only shrugged as if to say: "Hey, my job is translating Tibetan. That was in English, so it's your problem."

The Dalai Lama smiled gently at Jhampa and repeated again, more slowly, "I said: Do you know when you're going to die?"

Jhampa was still so surprised by what he was asked, much less its context, that all he could do was stare in return, finally uttering, "No." His Holiness started to laugh in a gentle way "You asked me a very big philosophical question," he acknowledged. "I say this to you: you must study. You must understand what the question you are asking is really about. You must find good teachers to help you."

The Dalai Lama, in fact, agreed to loan Jhampa the services of his own favored tutor, Kyabje Ling Rinpoche, as well as to assist the young monk personally when he could. When Jhampa stumbled out of the temple, his mind was reeling. He

understood already that His Holiness had tried to divert him from his intellectual pro-
clivities and had asked him about his own mortality as a way to keep him focused
on the fragility of life and the importance of appreciating every moment. This would
prove to be one of the most important lessons of Jhampa's life.

He would spend much of the next decade learning not only about Buddhism but also
the Tibetan language, [which] would allow him to communicate more directly with his
mentors and translate sacred texts into English. During this time, he spent four years in
a solitary retreat on a mountaintop, practicing meditation and purification rituals.

It was during this seclusion that three of Jhampa's teachers died. They had been
the cream of Buddhist meditators who had been driven from Tibet after the Chinese
invasion. Once they were gone, Jhampa decided it was time for him to continue his
own journey in the world as a teacher. He returned home to Canada, where he
established his own meditation center, later adding another in Central Mexico.

Jhampa reflects, "Lama Yeshe was only forty-nine years old when he died; he had a very damaged heart from rheumatic fever as a child. I was his secretary during the early years of our relationship. Lama Yeshe suffered terribly from heart pain but he never, ever complained. He was able to manage his pain and live his life to the fullest."

The Dalai Lama's comment to Jhampa, asking him whether he knew when he was going to die, is a very existential question. It reminds us that our tenure on Earth is relatively brief, that all of us are mortal, and that any of us could die at any moment. Rather than causing us to feel terrified by this prospect, the idea of death motivates us to appreciate every second and live as if there were no tomorrow. Impermanence is what makes a life—or anything else—so precious.

We asked Jhampa, "How does one find a purpose in life?" He answered by asking us two questions: "Are you happy?" and "Do you know when you are going to die?"

Are you satisfied with what you are doing with your life now and how you are living? Jhampa is concerned with not merely your own happiness but also what you are doing for others. What are you doing for your community? You may be living out the purpose of your life at this time. Your life might not look like Mother Teresa's or Lama Yeshe's, but it's your life, not theirs. Remember Mother Teresa's edict: "If you can't feed a hundred people, then feed just one!" Keep in mind that once you get above poverty level, money is not associated with happiness. When Jhampa had everything he ever wanted, he was still not content and was not living a purposeful life. Yet when his only possessions were a robe and a rice bowl, he felt a degree of satisfaction and happiness that was off the scale.

The Dalai Lama's question about knowing when we will die forces us to consider our own impermanence. What do you want to do with the limited time that is available to you? Are you pleased with how you are spending your time? What is the legacy that you are leaving behind? How are you living in the moment? What if the rest of your life was the best of your life? What would that look like?

It is hardly necessary to become a monk to find happiness or lead a significant life. Relationships and meaningful work are important features of a happy, satisfied, and significant life. Frivolous activities and superficial relationships get in the way. What is getting in your way as you move toward living out the purpose of your life?

Few of us are prepared to move to India, take vows as Tibetan monks or nuns, remain celibate, and spend our lives in solitary meditation in a monastery. Thus, the following question arises: "What can the rest of us learn from Jhampa's experience?"

The first thing is to become aware of how deeper, unconscious motives affect our life decisions and choices. Only after many years did Jhampa realize that one of his main attractions to the Buddhist way was feeling part of a fellowship of men, many of whom were significant father figures who filled a huge emotional and spiritual need. His yearning led him to his purpose in life. Even for those who don't yearn for a surrogate parent, enlightenment of any sort, spiritual or intellectual, is best facilitated under the guidance of a trained mentor. This can be a member of the clergy, a teacher, a coach, an artisan, or even an author, but it is best if it is someone who is well trained, who exhibits compassion and caring, and who lives his or her life in a way you wish to emulate.

If you are not clear about your purpose in life, could it be that you need to find good teachers to help you? Almost anyone who is passionate about his or her purpose in life will be delighted to share it with you; the price of admission is usually just your interest and your energy.

Pat found her mentor, Dr. Ed Jacobs, by showing up for extra practice sessions in graduate school. Her interest in becoming a better counselor caught Ed's attention, and he began inviting her along when he conducted trainings and workshops. Over the course of three years, Ed taught her about 90 percent of what she learned in her graduate studies. Simply following her interests led her to her mentor.

Jon was more deliberate. He "met" his mentor, Dr. Don Dinkmeyer, by reading his books. Jon was impressed by Dr. Dinkmeyer's work and even more impressed when he discovered that Dr. Dinkmeyer's name was one of the most respected in the field of psychology. It was clear to Jon that there was a lot to be learned from this man, so Jon took a job consulting under Dr. Dinkmeyer's supervision.

Finding a mentor or a teacher is often the result of simply following your interests, discovering a personality match, and feeling the energy of inspiration. Jhampa describes Lama Yeshe as a main source of inspiration in his life.

"I am in Mexico right now," Jhampa explained in an interview, "so I'm learning Spanish. Their [Mexicans'] word for 'meaningful' is *significado*. A life of significance. I believe that Lama Yeshe had found for himself a life of true significance. That is what made his life so meaningful to me and so many others."

Does your life have significance? If so, how does this significance relate to your purpose in life? If you believe that your life doesn't have significance, what is an action you can take to give it significance?

Exercise 22: **Passage Meditation**

While searching for the purpose of life, many of us have discovered that passage meditation, created by Eknath Easwaran, is very useful. "In passage meditation," Easwaran explains, "you choose a spiritual text or passage that embodies your highest ideals, memorize it, and then go through the words slowly, silently, and with as much concentration as possible. This method brings two important benefits. First, by training our mind to stay on the words of the passage, we gradually build the precious capacity to place our attention wherever we choose, and we begin to resemble and actually become whatever we give our attention to. As the inspired words from the great spiritual traditions of the world slowly come to life in us, they bring with them quiet joy, the capacity to face challenges squarely, and a deep sense of fulfillment."

A sample passage is the Prayer of St. Francis of Assisi:

Lord, make me an instrument of thy peace.
Where there is hatred, let me sow love;
Where there is injury, pardon;
Where there is doubt, faith;
Where there is despair, hope;
Where there is darkness, light;
Where there is sadness, joy.
O divine Master, grant that I may not so much seek
To be consoled as to console,
To be understood as to understand,
To be loved as to love;
For it is in giving that we receive;
It is in pardoning that we are pardoned;
It is in dying to self that we are born to eternal life.

Another example is "The Best" by Chinese poet Lao Tzu:

The best, like water,
Benefit all and do not compete.
They dwell in lowly spots that everyone else scorns.
Putting others before themselves,
They find themselves in the foremost place

And come very near to the Tao.
In their dwelling, they love the earth;
In their heart, they love what is deep;
In personal relationships, they love kindness;
In their words, they love truth.
In the world, they love peace.
In personal affairs, they love what is right.
In action, they love choosing the right time.
It is because they do not compete with others
That they are beyond the reproach of the world.

You may have your own sources to use in passage meditation. If not, Dr. Easwaran's *Timeless Wisdom* is a good sourcebook. Using inspirational messages trains your brain to focus on positive beliefs, which in turn can lead to positive actions. Living out the purpose of your life is active, not passive. It includes taking steps toward goals that are in line with your purpose. Actions have to be supported by the affirming belief that your life does have purpose as well as power.

Humanity needs your talents to be used in a meaningful manner. Even what you consider your least ability—for example, your attention, your interest, or your listening ear—can make an important difference in today's world. Using your talents in a significant way can also lead to your personal happiness. In the next chapter we will examine the connections among life purpose, happiness, and the end of loneliness.

8

Happiness, Purpose, and the End of Loneliness

I BELIEVE THE VERY PURPOSE OF
LIFE IS TO BE HAPPY.

—The Dalai Lama

Are you surprised to read this statement? We were, at first, because our Western minds immediately thought that making happiness our purpose in life seemed selfish and egocentric. When we looked at the statement through Buddhist eyes, however, we remembered that happiness is directly dependent on kindness, compassion, and caring for others.

Here's the rest of the quote: "From the very core of our being, we desire contentment. In my own limited experience I have found that the more we care for the happiness of others, the greater is our own sense of well-being."

It's easy to visualize the Dalai Lama smiling as he says that the purpose of life is to be happy, because we suspect that he has an ulterior motive. Who wouldn't want to be happy? If we are honest, most of us will admit that we strive for happiness every day. Why would we strive for misery or suffering?

His Holiness knows better than most that happiness, which encompasses contentment and well-being, is related to acts of goodwill and caring. His linking of happiness to the purpose of life may be like the statement of his that we mentioned earlier: "I'm not so concerned if you believe in reincarnation. I'm not so concerned if you believe in karma. What concerns me most is that you are compassionate; because if you have compassion you'll have good karma and a good reincarnation!" Similarly, if your purpose in life is to be happy, then you will care for others, because caring for others is what creates ultimate happiness as well as personal well-being—and personal well-being includes the absence of loneliness.

It's not just the Dalai Lama or Eastern spiritual traditions that maintain that caring for others is the primary key to happiness. Years of Western research have revealed the same: the single greatest predictor of personal happiness and well-being is investing in the welfare and happiness of others.

Martin Seligman, Dan Gilbert, and Mihaly Csikszentmihalyi are three leaders who have explored human behavior from the perspective of what makes us happy. Instead of focusing on mental illness or pathology, these groundbreaking researchers have spent decades looking at the factors that lead to contentment, joy, and even bliss. Their studies prove that using your time, attention, and talent in a way that improves the lives of others is the most consistent path to personal happiness.

This doesn't mean that we all have to take vows of poverty and move to India or even become full-time volunteers, and it certainly doesn't mean that we have to give up the many fun activities we enjoy. Golf, gardening, or a bike ride can make you happy and provide energy for the tasks that ultimately improve the lives of others. Let's take a closer look at how this works.

Although it is true that using your talent to better someone else's life is a direct route to happiness, there are other ways to get there. Many activities create happiness: increasing your income above poverty level, gaining freedom from oppression, being in nature, petting cats and dogs, hanging out with happy people, dancing, singing, playing music, exercising, and mastery (getting better at something). All of these enjoyable activities lift your spirits and energize you—that's the nature of happiness.

Nevertheless, these activities will help to eliminate loneliness only if they ultimately address the sources of loneliness posed in the five questions we asked in Part II: Who am I? Am I connected? Am I living in community? Are my talents being utilized in meaningful work? Am I living out the purpose of my life? The joy you get from playing golf, for example, should fit who you are, strengthen your closest connections with others, leave enough time and energy to make a contribution to your community, increase the energy you need to use your skills in meaningful work, and add meaning to your life.

Fun activities fuel our engines for finer acts—acts of kindness, support, caring, and compassion. The happiness that eliminates loneliness cannot benefit you alone; it must ultimately enhance the lives of others. When your happiness is intertwined with the happiness of others, this is the beginning of the end of loneliness.

Truly happy and contented people know who they are and are diligent in living out their core values daily. They invest time and energy in relationships in order to develop and maintain close connections with significant people. They participate in the improvement of the communities to which they belong. They utilize their talents in meaningful work—sometimes they get paid for this work, sometimes they don't. They have fun. They find ways to enjoy life. They have the sense that their lives have purpose because each day their actions have meaning to them and to others.

As time goes by, their relationships grow deeper with meaning, and loneliness recedes farther into the background. They strive to be happy, for happy people are rarely lonely; like the Dalai Lama, they attract people and their spirit is contagious. They stay mindful of the time and the energy that is required to maintain a life of purpose. When they get off track, they feel the discontent and ask themselves the five questions.

Even after years of practice, both of us still have to be mindful to live lives of purpose and keep loneliness at bay. It is an intentional path, and some days are easier than others. We hope that this book will make your path easier and support you when you struggle as we have struggled.

Jon's Happiness

Happiness was always part of my life purpose, but after India I understood that I had been looking for happiness in the wrong places. Happiness had always been tied so closely with achievement. I was attached to success. I realized that the recognition I received from my accomplishments always seemed so much more important than anything else. I remember receiving awards with cash prizes and valuing the plaque or the trophy more than the cash prize or whatever I had contributed.

Since my trip to India, I find happiness in doing what I set out to do and in focusing on creating the self-fulfillment that comes from living my dreams or my purpose. I am much more satisfied with giving and mentoring, whereas before I was giving to get. Recognition and status have become less important than the process and the contribution. I notice that I now feel genuine happiness for others who receive recognition and experience compassion for those who are struggling. I have discovered that my loneliness had a big component of insecurity and self-doubt, which was reinforced by focusing on myself. I didn't really believe that I was okay or worthy. I felt like an impostor trying to prove that he belonged.

After my trip to India, I began to know and understand myself, which has led to an acceptance of my strengths as well as my weaknesses. I find that I am less defensive and more willing to accept responsibility for my role in things. Alfred Adler called this the "courage to be imperfect." I finally learned that what I was doing wasn't the problem; it was my motivation, or why I was doing it. I was attached to the recognition, not the act of kindness or generosity. I guess I was living out what I thought was my purpose but my emphasis was in the wrong place.

Pat's Happiness

I have never thought of happiness as being linked to my purpose in life. I would say that my purpose in life is to do my best to make the world a better place; my goals include using my particular talents in a manner that helps others. Before my trip to India, my life was compartmentalized. My work life was channeled toward helping others, but the rest of my life was incongruent, and the incongruity was depressing.

Before India, my answers to the five questions would not have had the clarity that they have today. On a scale of 1 to 10, with 1 being unclear and 10 being very clear, my answers would have looked like this:

Who am I?	5	(I had a lot to learn about myself.)
Am I connected?	6	(I wasn't being entirely honest in my connections.)
Am I in community?	4	(My efforts were erratic and unclear.)
Are my talents utilized in work?	8	(I sublimated other needs in work.)
Do I live a purposeful life?	6	(My life lacked clear purpose.)

When I returned from India I had my work cut out for me. I had to change a lot of the basic structure of my support system, my lifestyle, my relationships, and my mental attitude. I've been busy; but it's been well worth the effort. My life looks very different than it did a few short years ago. Some of the people have changed, and how I spend my time, money, and energy have changed. I am closer to living out the purpose of my life because now my life is simpler, quieter, more congruent with my core values, and more conducive to using my talents in a meaningful way. I have the time and the energy to improve my close connections as well as my relationship to the broader community.

I'm not finished, and there's plenty of room for improvement, but I'm happy and I make time for fun every chance I get. I have time for meaningful endeavors and the people I love, and I am no longer lonely.

Happiness Saboteurs

Whether you have made happiness your purpose in life, it is probably safe to assume that being happy is at least a goal, and we want to support you in attaining that goal, because happiness is a powerful antidote to loneliness. It draws people to you, and it generates the energy that is required to develop meaningful connections and live a purposeful life. We have already listed several ways to increase happiness; now we want to help you stay on track by calling your attention to the saboteurs of happiness. There are two major ones: resisting change and confusing happiness with pleasure.

Resisting Change

You may have habits and routines that prevent you from being happy—for example, getting too little sleep (a good night's sleep is the single greatest predictor of happiness on any given day), avoiding mood-elevating exercise, spending time with critical or negative people, eating food that makes you feel good in the moment but crummy later, or indulging in time-wasting activities.

Regardless of what habit you attempt to change, it is realistic to expect resistance. You should expect resistance when you have to set aside an enjoyable task to get to bed earlier or when you say, "That's enough work for today; everything else will have to wait." You might feel guilty or bargain with yourself by saying, "Just this one night." If you do manage to get to bed earlier on one or two nights, you might find yourself sliding back into the old late-night habit later in the week.

Change brings resistance sooner or later; therefore, you must be ready to face the resistance by doing the right thing. Listen to the resistance but go to bed anyway. If you are ignoring your need to exercise, acknowledge the desire to sit on the couch but get up and take a walk. Be mindful of the resistance to change; feel the feeling, then do the right thing.

Other changes that you need to make to increase your level of happiness may meet with resistance from others, such as limiting the time you spend with someone who is critical or negative. You may get a backlash or complaints from this person as well as pressure to reinstate your former habits. Again, you must recognize resistance when it shows up and learn to manage your reaction to it.

This is one reason that we have included exercises in each chapter; you have to be prepared mentally and emotionally to change your life behaviorally. Giving in to the resistance to change will keep you stuck where you are. If you are happy where you are now, keep on doing what you are doing, but if you want something different, you are going to have to do something different, despite the resistance.

Confusing Happiness with Pleasure

Another common way to sabotage happiness is to confuse it with pleasure. Pleasure feels good in the moment; happiness feels good in the memory. Thinking about the doughnut you ate this morning might make you hungry, but it doesn't warm your heart. In contrast, recalling a time when you made someone happy is just as sweet and gratifying now as it was then. Pleasure is transitory; happiness is timeless. Pleasure is for now; happiness is forever.

The evolutionary purpose behind many of life's pleasures is survival. Activities that support life, like eating, resting, and mating, are reinforced with dopamine, the feel-good neurotransmitter that makes you want more. Eating *anything*, for example, releases dopamine; the pleasure from the experience is designed to ensure nourishment and ward off starvation. Sex is another feel-good experience; because it is directly related to the procreation of the species, it, too, is therefore about survival. But meeting your sexual or other biological needs, no matter how enjoyable, will not eliminate loneliness.

Pleasure can sabotage happiness also because it is difficult to regulate. A certain amount of need gratification is necessary to survive, but how much is enough? Because many pleasures—like eating, resting, having sex, or hanging out with friends—involve meeting your biological needs, you can't regulate the need by giving up the pleasure altogether. We all have biological needs, and happiness is dependent on having those needs met first. It's tough to be happy when you are hungry, thirsty, or isolated, but you have to know where to draw the line.

It is interesting to note that the pleasures associated with biological needs are actually an elimination of negative experiences: eating eliminates hunger, orgasm eliminates sexual tension, sleeping eliminates exhaustion, and socializing eliminates loneliness. The gratification, however, is proportional to the need; the greater the pain of the need, the greater the pleasure in meeting the need. The hungrier you are, the more pleasure you get from eating. If you eat when you are not hungry (when you have no need for the dopamine high), the pleasure is minimal. You have to eat more to get even a modicum of pleasure from it.

This may partly explain why 64 percent of Americans are overweight and 34 percent are obese. An additional hazard created by eating beyond your need is craving. When you are eating just for the dopamine high and not to meet a biological need, you begin to crave food when you are not hungry because you need more and more food to get the least bit of pleasure. Indulging yourself with pleasure purely for pleasure's sake produces suffering, because it chips away at your self esteem and core values. Who wants to be known as a self-indulgent consumer? Who wants to be remembered as a person obsessed with his or her own pleasure?

Confusing happiness and pleasure has another hidden saboteur: need displacement. This occurs when you have one need but settle for another as a substitute; for example, displacing intimacy with sex. If you long for loving emotional contact but settle for sex just to have some form of connection, over time you lose track of the real need for intimacy and you start to crave sex. Craving is a sure sign you are off track. When you are thinking about your next sexual experience right after you've had sex, this is a heads-up that you are on the wrong track.

Another example is the displacement of social contact with hours of mind-numbing television or video games. Before long you are glued to a machine, craving more time—but you can't get loving emotional intimacy, the kind that brings tears to your eyes and creates limbic resonance, from a machine. Displacing your needs with momentary pleasure can lead to suffering and loneliness.

Pleasure is important when it is connected to authentic need gratification, but it should be a means to an end that is congruent with your core values. Pleasure should also support the relationships that mean the most to you. Pleasure should not interfere with your talents being utilized in meaningful work or your ability to live out the purpose of your life. Pleasure should always lead you toward significant connection and away from loneliness.

From MySpace to Your Space

Because of the enormous pleasure that many of us get from technology in today's world, we feel the need to address this issue separately. If trends continue, many of you will be reading this material on a gadget instead of in a clothbound or paperback book; and even if you're reading a book, you probably have your cell phone and/or a computer nearby. You might even be reading it on your cell phone. We are indeed living in a new world, with even more technological innovations just around the corner, such as a phone that can be implanted in a tooth, and contact lenses that can project a computer image in front of your eyes. It boggles the mind but titillates us at the same time.

MySpace became the most popular social media website in June 2006, and by August of that year it registered its 100 millionth account. Less than two years later it was surpassed by Facebook. By the time you are reading this book, both of those could easily be eclipsed by yet another site, game, blog, or chat, because the human brain loves stimulation.

Basically, you are born with a brain but no mind; the mind is formed by stimulation coming in through the senses, creating neural pathways that translate into memories, sensations, perceptions, and knowledge. A brain deprived of stimulation fails to organize. An infant deprived of stimulation fails to thrive and dies. We crave stimulation; it is a biological need. Sensory deprivation drives us crazy.

Nevertheless, seeking stimulation beyond your need can sabotage happiness and interfere with your life purpose if it pulls you away from your core values, causes disconnection in your relationships, or prevents your talents from being utilized in meaningful work. Let's take a closer look at the issues related to technological stimulation.

Recalibrating Your Stimulation Set Point

Past experiences set the standard by which we judge new experiences. Pleasure and satisfaction lie in the ratio of what you expect to what you get. Just a few years ago a good week of entertainment might include going to a movie, watching some TV, maybe playing a computer game in the evening, or possibly getting together with a friend or two. That was considered rather stimulating.

Now we expect entertainment every day, most of the day. In today's world, technology has provided the means for constant novelty and stimulation. As we write this book, twenty-four hours' worth of new YouTube videos are being uploaded every minute—in HD and 3D. The site gets 2 billion views *per day*. At your fingertips is a constant stream of new stimulation. It's now possible to fill every moment with novel input—the brain loves novelty—because paying attention to novelty is also connected to survival.

Our brain is programmed to pay special attention to anything new or different to determine if it is friend or foe. A new plant needs scrutiny to eliminate the possibility of poison; a new animal deserves observation to learn its feeding habits (and to see if you are on the menu). Novelty gets us to buy a new shirt when we have thirty-nine perfectly good ones at home. Novelty and stimulation are difficult to regulate because they support survival. Technology puts an endless stream of new stimulation at our fingertips 24/7, and it's almost impossible to be in business in the twenty-first century without using some form of technology. Even if you can be in business without it, you probably still want it.

The problem with imbibing in constant technological stimulation, other than the waste of time, is the adaptation-level principle. Your brain becomes accustomed to relentless input, and that becomes the norm—that is, the set point for stimulation. Once your stimulation set point is calibrated toward a constant flow of entertainment, anything less seems boring, and when you get bored, you can immediately remedy the boredom with new stimulation. It makes you wonder whether real people with real stories can compete.

We are talking about rather benign forms of stimulation here. What if you shift gears to sexual stimulation, such as sensual or erotic material? Each picture recalibrates the stimulation set point. This, by the way, is how most people get in way over their heads with pornography. Few people start out looking at hard-core porn. Normal curiosity leads to one picture; your brain adapts, then you look at another and another. Each subsequent picture has to be novel and a little more stimulating than the last to get the dopamine effect. Before you know it, soft-core porn doesn't provide much of a thrill, and you must move to hard-core to get stimulation. How can a real live partner ever compete with the endless supply of novelty coupled with sexual stimulation?

The stimulation set point principle applies to most of life's pleasures. If you got $100 for your last birthday, you expect at least $100 or more on your next birthday. Any less will not give you the same pleasure. Satisfaction from an experience is directly related to a comparison with our prior experiences of the same nature. When you got the $100, that amount became your expectation; it recalibrated your pleasure set point. If you get $25 the next time, you won't get much pleasure from it.

Seeking pleasure beyond need, whether it involves technological stimulation or strawberry sundaes, sets us up for disappointment and craving, sabotages happiness, and increases our chances of being lonely.

We are going into detail about the lure of pleasure-seeking behavior because it takes up an enormous amount of time and is a common barrier to true happiness. We spend more time seeking pleasure and/or stimulation by being tuned in to some form of technology (Internet, phone, TV, radio, iPod), than anything else *other than breathing*. That's right—we spend more time plugged in to technology than sleeping, working, shopping, or socializing.

We are so hooked on technological stimulation that we even put our jobs at risk. Thirty percent of 1,500 companies surveyed said that they had had to fire someone because of inappropriate use of the Internet. Many of us have recalibrated our stimulation set points to such high levels that it greatly interferes with our purposes in life.

If your primary purpose in life is pleasure-seeking, self-gratification, self-indulgence, self-focus, or hedonism, happiness will elude you. Hedonism is all about you; happiness is about others.

Shifting from Pleasure to Happiness

How do you shift from pleasure-seeking to pursuing happiness? First, know the components of happiness, and second, make a plan and follow it. One of the most common observations people make about the Dalai Lama is how happy he is. As we write this chapter, His Holiness is celebrating his seventy-fifth birthday.

In an interview scheduled to honor this occasion, Barkha Dutt from New Delhi Television (NDTV) commented, "Many people describe you as twinkly-eyed. You know, there is a twinkle in your eyes, you are always laughing, you make us laugh, you make everybody who meets you happier, calmer. Do you always internally feel as positive as you appear, or do you feel the need to appear more positive than you feel because of the millions who follow you everywhere?"

The Dalai Lama responded that he does not feel pressure to appear more positive than he feels. His internal state is quite calm. He added that we are all the same and are therefore quite capable of feeling this way, too.

If we are all the same (*Homo sapiens*), how do we create happiness? There are two major ways: by cultivating positive emotions and by using your particular skills for the good of others. It's no coincidence that these two choices go hand in hand. Research indicates that positive emotions lead to positive acts, and vice versa. Doing good makes you feel good, and feeling good makes you do good. We've talked extensively about doing good and using your talents for the good of others, so now let's focus on cultivating positive emotions.

Cultivating Positive Emotions

You might be surprised to realize how many people believe that they have no control over their emotions. "That's just the way I am" is used to excuse anger, criticism, defensiveness, fear, suspicion, and many other emotions. The truth is that you can choose how you feel. You can't always choose what happens to you or how others treat you, but you can choose how you respond, internally as well as externally. You can choose to focus on positive emotions at any time. We are not talking about walking around in denial or with your head in the clouds. We are talking about choosing your state of mind, choosing the thoughts you think and the feelings you feel, and taking responsibility for cultivating a positive internal state.

According to the Dalai Lama, all negative emotions are based on ignorance, which is the misconception of the true nature of reality. These emotions therefore have no basis in reality. Positive emotions, in contrast, are grounded in reality and are life-supporting. By training the mind to focus on the positive, we can develop an inner discipline. Having inner discipline means confronting our negative states of mind and transforming them into more positive states. The goal is to develop a calm, peaceful, and stable state of mind that you can access at will. This is achieved by simply watching negative states of mind, knowing that they will pass, and realizing that they are feelings and not facts. We all have a full range of emotions; we can choose whether or when to use them.

The idea is to free ourselves from negativity by developing and cultivating positive thoughts and emotions and then living and acting from that state. Positive states can be an antidote to negativity. By coming from a state of joy, love, or enthusiasm, you can neutralize anger, hatred, or apathy on an individual level. The goal then is to develop habits out of those positive states to make them the predominant state. Positive states lead to happiness, and happiness provides the energy to lead a life of purpose in which there is no loneliness.

We think that the best way to cultivate positive emotions is to meditate, concentrate, recall, and record positive feelings such as love, kindness, compassion, and generosity, because these include other people. This can be done by remembering a time when you felt any of these emotions and rehearsing them over and over in your mind.

Pat remembers an early incident involving compassion. She was about twelve years old and was making the long trip from West Virginia to Georgia on a Greyhound bus to visit her grandfather for the summer. She was by herself and was looking out the window as the bus stopped to pick up passengers in a small town in southern West Virginia. Among the people waiting to board the bus was a boy about ten and a man who seemed to be his father. The man was obviously drunk—so drunk that at one point he staggered and fell facedown on the pavement, seriously striking the left side of his forehead. Blood was flowing down his face as he attempted to get up but couldn't. The little boy tried several times to help him up, but he wasn't strong enough, so he went over to the bus driver to ask for help.

Pat will never forget the look on that young boy's face as he pleaded for help. She felt such compassion that she even thought about getting off the bus to try to help. She had been in a similar situation with her own mother just a few years earlier and knew firsthand the intense feelings the boy must be having. Fortunately, a man and a woman came to the rescue. They helped the father get up, got wet towels to clean and soothe the injury, and gave the boy money to make a call from a nearby pay phone. They were sitting with the father and son as the bus drove away.

Reading about this event might generate feelings of compassion in you. Take a moment to imagine wanting to help the young boy or the man, or imagine how gratifying it was for the man and the woman to help them. Just put yourself in their shoes for a moment. Visualize reaching out to the boy or the man. Recalling acts of love, kindness, or compassion for others—even ones in which you were not involved—can cultivate positive emotions, which you can choose to feel at any moment. These positive emotions, research shows, inspire positive acts, and positive acts lead to connection and away from loneliness. The following exercise provides guidelines for increasing positive emotions.

Exercise 23:
Cultivating Positive Emotions

This simple meditation is designed to increase positive emotions and broaden your repertoire of affirmative responses to life events. Positive people are happier people; happiness draws people to you and provides a source of energy for living out a purposeful life. A positive mental attitude is a powerful resource that you can access at any time. We are going to begin by inviting you to increase your mental measure of three positive emotions: love, kindness, and compassion. We choose these because they are the most likely to include other people and lead to connection. We suggest that as you visualize and meditate, you choose examples that include acts involving others.

Remembering Love

Sit in an upright position, close your eyes, and focus on your breath. Let each exhalation remind you to relax, let go of passing thoughts, and focus on your breath. Once you feel relaxed and focused, recall a time that includes an act of love. Take whatever time you need to bring this loving act into focus. Remember the time of love: see the scene before you, hear the sounds of love, feel the feelings of this time, and taste the taste and smell the smells that come with this time.

Pay attention as you feel the love. Feel it in your body and let it expand. As you breath in and out, let the word *love* go with each exhalation. As you exhale love, see it fill the air around you. Watch as it expands and moves out into the world. See others, even strangers, being touched by that love. See it finding people you know and care for; see it touching them with love. Stay with this experience as long as you want. Enjoy filling your heart and your mind with love.

Remembering Kindness

Sit in an upright position, close your eyes, and focus on your breath. Let each exhalation remind you to relax, let go of passing thoughts, and focus on your breath. Once you feel relaxed and focused, recall a time that includes an act of kindness— toward you or toward another person or group of people. Take whatever time you need to bring this act of kindness into focus. Remember the kind act: see the scene before you, hear the sounds of kindness, feel the feelings of kindness, and taste the taste and smell the smells that come with this act of kindness.

Pay attention as you feel the kindness. Feel it in your body and let it expand. As you breath in and out, let the word *kindness* go with each exhalation. As you exhale kindness, see it fill the air around you. Watch as it expands and moves out into the world. See others, even strangers, being touched by kindness. See it finding people you know and care for; see it touching them with kindness. Stay with this experience as long as you want. Enjoy filling your heart and your mind with kindness.

Remembering Compassion

Sit in an upright position, close your eyes, and focus on your breath. Let each exhalation remind you to relax, let go of passing thoughts, and focus on your breath. Once you feel relaxed and focused, recall a time that includes an act of compassion: an act designed to ease someone's suffering, either your own or another's. Take whatever time you need to bring this act of compassion into focus. Remember the compassionate act: see the scene before you, hear the sounds of compassion, feel the feelings of compassion, and taste the taste and smell the smells that come with this act of compassion.

Pay attention as you feel the compassion. Feel it in your body and let it expand. As you breathe in and out, let the word *compassion* go with each exhalation. As you exhale compassion, see it fill the air around you. Watch as it expands and moves out into the world. See others, even strangers, being touched by compassion. See it finding people you know and care for; see it touching them with compassion. Stay with this experience as long as you want. Enjoy filling your heart and your mind with compassion.

Using Your Skills to Help Others

The Dalai Lama advises, "We must learn to work not just for our own individual self, family, or nation, but for the benefit of all mankind. Universal responsibility is the best foundation both for our personal happiness and for world peace."

Happiness is up to you, but it's not about you. To be happy, you much reach outside yourself, beyond your own needs and into the needs of others. You have special skills, talents, and capabilities; using them to help others is the key to happiness. You may have the gift of gab and with it the ability to make people feel welcome and included. You may have a talent for music and taking others' minds to a happy place. You may have the ability to cook a fine meal and serve it to others. You may have discretionary time to clean up trash and improve the aesthetics of the environment. You may be a fine listener and a healer of souls. You may have a car and be able to drive meals to people who can't get out.

Only you know your abilities. How are you using these to make the world a better place? How are you using your talents to improve the lives of others? Consistent acts of kindness, helpfulness, and compassion create a happy life.

When we conduct workshops on developing meaningful connection, we often ask the participants to think of an example of when they used their particular talents or skills to improve someone else's life—something they didn't get paid to do. It's interesting to watch the individual reactions to this exercise. When we first suggest it, we get blank stares, silence, and even embarrassment, but when the participants finally start telling their stories and sharing examples, the atmosphere changes. There are sometimes tears of joy, frequent laughter, and a lot of smiling.

At one particular workshop, a woman named Carla told a story about a ritual she began with her housekeeper, Nellie, years ago. It was Friday, the day on which Nellie came to clean. Carla was preparing lunch for herself and suddenly got the idea to invite Nellie to eat with her.

Recognizing how hard Nellie worked, Carla thought that she might like a break in the middle of the day to rest and renew her energy. In addition, Carla decided that she would make lunch not just a meal but an occasion, almost like a party. She got out the best china and crystal, used colorful place mats and napkins, and cut fresh flowers from her garden to put on the table. When the two women sat down together, they held hands and said a blessing to give thanks for food as well as the fellowship. They both enjoyed the experience so much that they repeated it the following week.

It was interesting to watch the other participants as Carla told her story. At the end she added that she and Nellie were still practicing the ritual years later, and the beaming expression on her face showed that the happiness was still fresh. We looked around, and it was plain to see that this small act of kindness kindled warm feelings throughout the room. Just hearing Carla talk about her experience and sensing her joy created a contact high; the feelings were contagious. We reminded everyone that the purpose of the exercise was to experience firsthand how good it feels to use your particular talents in a loving way.

Finding happiness in life may begin with a simple act of kindness. When your actions bring you joy and reflect your core values, you will be headed in the right direction toward your purpose in life. There are so many people waiting on your time and talents. When was the last time you made someone happy?

Part Three

Leaving Loneliness Behind

There is an end to loneliness. Hopefully by the time you read this you have experienced the truth in this statement. As you live out each day exemplifying your core values; as your behavior becomes more compassionate and kind; as you strengthen your connection to other people and invest in the welfare of the wider community—the weight of loneliness will lift. As you apply your talents to meaningful work and your life takes on deeper meaning, loneliness will recede into the past and a brighter, more contented future will unfold.

We are confident about the journey away from loneliness we have outlined in this book and if you follow the path we've laid out, we believe you'll understand it is possible to never be lonely again. To support you in this continued journey we offer two more chapters; the first is about the Middle Way, a common sense approach to keep you realistic and balanced as you move away from loneliness. The second chapter is a reminder that you get to choose how you respond to the life you are living—your choice.

9

The Middle Way

A BALANCED AND SKILLFUL APPROACH TO LIFE,
TAKING CARE TO AVOID EXTREMES,
BECOMES A VERY IMPORTANT FACTOR IN CONDUCTING
ONE'S EVERYDAY EXPERIENCE.

—The Dalai Lama

You may have read the book *Siddhartha* in high school, in college, or on your own, as we did, but the lessons from it take on a whole new meaning after being in India.

The story is that Maya, the mother of Siddhartha Gautama, who later became the Buddha, was told shortly before the birth of her son that he would become either a great emperor or a great spiritual teacher. Suddhodana, Siddhartha's father, fearful that his son would leave home to fulfill his destiny as a spiritual teacher, used his great wealth and power to sequester Siddhartha behind the palace walls and distract him with a life of luxury. Suddhodana filled the palace compound with only smiling, healthy, young people; he was worried that if his son ever encountered suffering, illness, and aging, he would be filled with compassion and compelled to fulfill his destiny as a spiritual teacher rather than as emperor.

Siddhartha therefore spent the first twenty-nine years of his life in lavish surroundings, isolated from the rest of the world. As pleasant as this might sound, however, Siddhartha was unfulfilled by the luxury and self-indulgence; he grew restless and increasingly curious about what lay outside the palace walls. Finally, curiosity got the best of him, and with the help of his personal aide, he ventured outside, where he encountered elderly people, sick people, suffering people, and dying people.

Shocked and deeply moved by this new reality, Siddhartha returned to the palace to contemplate the human condition. After a period, he again went outside the palace, where he met a religious man who inspired him to believe that there might be a spiritual solution to life's suffering. Motivated by this belief, Siddhartha made a radical decision to leave the palace as well as his family, which by now included a wife and an infant son, and go in search of spiritual truth.

Siddhartha began to look for teachers who could lead him on a path to the end of suffering; being a very gifted student, he readily found them. One teacher taught him how to enter a profound state of trance, another trained him to experience a state of nothingness, and a third introduced him to a state of bliss. He was so extraordinary that his teachers wanted him to become *their* teacher, but Siddhartha refused. Altered states, even those of ecstasy, were not his goal, for he could clearly see that when he moved from the trance state into normal consciousness, the fundamental problems of life—hunger, sickness, aging, and death—were still there, unresolved.

Continuing his search for the answers to life's suffering, Siddhartha turned next to asceticism, the practice of drastically reducing one's needs. He learned to slow his breathing and reduce his intake of oxygen, and he learned to deny his need for sleep and stay awake for extended periods. He learned to reduce his food intake and ultimately limited his nourishment to minuscule proportions. He is said to have existed on one grain of rice a day.

Before long, he was exhausted and emaciated, his hair began to fall out, he didn't even have the strength to sit up, and he was close to death. Fortunately, before death claimed his life, he realized that this extreme self-denial was futile and was not producing the results he longed for. So he abandoned asceticism with the clear realization that any extreme way of life, whether decadence or denial, would not work. A middle way must be found.

The story of Siddhartha, the Buddha, is the story of a man who gave up riches for rags and then returned to a life of moderation. He recognized the consequences of extreme living and abandoned it before dying and not living out the purpose of his life. Being mindful saved his life, and from this experience he was inspired to live a life according to what he called the Middle Way, which became a vital part of his legacy.

This Middle Way, which calls for a life of mindfulness, reason, and balance, is essential for continuing on your path away from loneliness. As you address the five questions we've posed in this book—Who am I? Am I connected? Am I living in community? Are my talents utilized in meaningful work? Am I living out the purpose of my life?—we invite you to find your answers in mindful moderation. This means avoiding extremes and finding comfort in balance. Earlier in the book we noted that eradicating loneliness doesn't require you to be a saint like Mother Teresa or take a vow of poverty and devote your entire life to serving others. For most of us this would be extreme—leaving no time or energy for other aspects of life.

Balance is a major key to never being lonely again; if you focus on any one of the five questions to the exclusion of the others, it can cause imbalance. For example, if you focus too much on connecting to those close to you, it may leave little or no time for making a living or using your talents in meaningful work. If you spend four nights a week volunteering in the community, how will you nurture your closest relationships? The Middle Way includes being aware of the consequences of your behavior and creating a life of mindful moderation.

Extremism in any form is more likely to create loneliness than eliminate it, because extremists frighten and sometimes embarrass other people. The behavior of extremists seems out of balance and unpredictable, and we can't count on reason to stabilize the decision making of such people. The unpredictability creates tension, so we ultimately avoid it. Likewise, we are uncomfortable when people go to extremes by either overemphasizing or underemphasizing one of the key areas of life—for example, a person who is rigidly honest when silence or restraint would be more kind or considerate, or someone whose core value of loving applies only to a small, select group of people.

Perhaps you've had the experience of someone taking your friendship to an extreme—trying to get all of his or her needs met from you alone and being jealous of your other friends. This extreme expectation is out of balance with the nature of friendship and not representative of the Middle Way. On the contrary, you may know someone who claims to be your friend yet does not show up when you need him or her or who refuses to provide support on an ongoing basis. Neither extreme will nurture the friendship; the Middle Way of connection lies somewhere in between.

It's important to note that the Middle Way does not mean compromise. In compromise, no one gets his or her needs met. The Middle Way is about striking a reasonable balance in all five areas of life, living in moderation, and avoiding extreme actions.

Cultural Challenges for the Middle Way

It's interesting to go about life in Dharamsala, because that place is truly one of the crossroads of the world. Every day you meet someone from a culture different from your own. You often meet people who have taken a month, three months, six months, or even a year off from work to travel and explore. It seems so civilized to balance work with time off, but as Westerners from the United States, we marvel at this practice, because the first thought that follows a decision to take even a month off in today's job market is *If I took a month off, my job would be gone when I got back. If I left, they'd figure out how to get along without me, and that would be one less person on the payroll.* We cannot discount the truth in this belief, and if that represents your thinking, we want to suggest that there may be more of a Middle Way in the area of work than you realize.

A friend of ours, Jeannette, is a consultant for large banks that hold derivatives, the complicated securitized mortgages that few of us ordinary people understand. During the past two years, her work expectations literally spun out of control. What she was required to do to complete the job was not only out of balance, it left no time for the rest of her life. Finally, Jeannette said, "Enough! I'm done. I can't do this anymore." She told her boss that she was quitting. After thinking about it, the boss made a reasonable decision and came back and said, "If you can't do it, our system is wrong. Make me an offer." Jeannette made an offer (fortunately, she'd already thought about it); the boss accepted, and both the policy and her job description were changed.

We are not naive enough to believe that this will happen in every situation. In addition, we recognize that the Middle Way is more difficult in some cultures than in others. For example, there's a saying in the United States that "You can't be too thin or too rich," and because physical appearance and monetary wealth are so revered, it's very difficult to resist the pressure to define yourself by what you have or don't have. The economic divide has grown so deep and wide that economists are publicly decrying the decline of the middle class; people are now either rich or poor.

It's as though our all-or-nothing thinking has created a culture of extremes, with fewer and fewer of us in the middle class *or* the Middle Way. This extreme living is partly due to the fact that our happiness is trained to rise and fall in accordance with the Dow Jones average. The U.S. economy is based on the gross national product (GNP); our lives are bent on acquiring goods, money, and power.

In the kingdom of Bhutan, a tiny nation in the Himalaya Mountains between China and India, the economy is based on gross national happiness (GNH)! The values of the Bhutanese are focused on the ecology, cultural climate, community, health, vitality, and psychological well-being, and the people make their life decisions with these values in mind. They recognize that happiness has very little to do with money.

Of course, most of us don't live in Bhutan, so we will have to be reasonable and intentional to create a life in line with the Middle Way. Let's look at three processes that will assist you in creating a life of balance: right view, right concentration, and right mindfulness.

Right View

Jeannette was able to negotiate a more reasonable job expectation because she recognized that her job requirements had become extreme. Working long hours left little or no time for the other parts of her life. Her relationships suffered, her health suffered, she was exhausted, and she found it increasingly difficult to maintain a positive attitude. Then she had a "lightbulb moment": First, she saw the reality of her life— that her lifestyle was out of balance and would never lead to happiness. Second, she realized the impermanence of worldly goods—that no luxury she could obtain with the money she was making was worth the time and energy it was costing her. Third, she got a clear vision of what reasonable work would look like; she could see the Middle Way. When her boss said, "Make me an offer," Jeannette was ready with a response, and it did not include self-denial or self-indulgence. It was sensible, practical, and in balance with her needs as well as the needs of the job.

With right view, Jeannette got an objective look at her life, and in that lightbulb moment she saw how out of balance her work had become. She realized that the other areas of her life were being neglected and that her lifestyle no longer represented her core values. With

this realistic perspective, she realigned her life toward the Middle Way.
We want to give you an opportunity to get an objective look at your life
right now through an exercise.

Exercise 24: Right View: Seeing Yourself from Another's Point of View

Sit in a comfortable position with an erect posture. Close your eyes and begin to
focus on your breath. With each exhalation, just let go and relax.

As you continue to relax, imagine for the moment that you are viewing your own
life from a close friend's vantage point. This friend is able to see your life up close
and personal.

What core values would your friend see in you? How would your friend describe
you as a person? What would your friend notice about you and your closest relationships? How much support do you have? How much support do you give others? How
involved are you in your community? How would your friend describe you as a neighbor? What would your friend say about your work? Does your work utilize your talents
in a meaningful way? Does your work allow for time and energy to be spent nurturing your closest relationships as well as investing in the community? Finally, what
would your friend say about you and your purpose in life? Is your purpose clear? Are
you following your purpose?

Sometimes right view is best seen from the eyes of others—at least initially. It's
difficult to be objective about yourself, but the more you practice this objectivity and
reasonable thinking, the more clarity you will have.

The Benefits of Right View

In addition to helping you to attain objectivity, right view includes
gaining control of your thoughts and maintaining a positive state of
mind, regardless of the reality of life. You cannot always control what
circumstances befall you, but you can control how you view those circumstances. Right view means that you remain objective, you see the
facts, and you maintain a positive outlook, avoiding extremes in thinking and feeling as well as in attitude. It's not that you live in denial;
rather, you focus on thoughts that lead to a productive outcome and
that are in line with your core values.

Near the end of our visit with His Holiness, our friend and colleague Addison asked this question: "Given all the death, destruction, war, and poverty in the world, how do you keep a positive outlook on life?" Without batting an eye, the Dalai Lama said, "It's not what I see." If you know anything about the Dalai Lama, you understand that he is well-informed; when he says, "It's not what I see," he doesn't mean that he is not aware of the suffering around the world. He simply chooses right view, to focus on the positive aspects of life.

When you have right view—that is, a reasonable positive outlook— whether you say it or just think it, you will draw others to you. We enjoy the company of people who think and feel positively, because they make us feel good and we can trust them to maintain an affirmative approach to life regardless of the circumstances. This is the kind of person you want to live with, socialize with, and work with. On the contrary, we avoid the company of people who think negatively or harbor negative emotions, because they make us feel negative and they bring out the worst in us.

According to psychologist Elaine Hatfield, human emotions are contagious through the function of mirror neurons. This emotional contagion explains why being around an angry person can make you angry and why living with a depressed person can make you depressed— we influence and are influenced by others' emotions. You can certainly try to keep your attitude positive even when you are in the company of a negative person, but it takes energy to offset negative emotions and keep your defenses alert. You have to constantly be on guard lest your emotions go down with the ship.

If you harbor negative thoughts or focus on negative feelings, others will not be attracted to you, nor will they easily engage with you. Friendship and connection is far more difficult when negative feelings are part of the discourse, because we constantly have to be on guard against emotional contagion. Think about it: most of us won't willingly interact with someone if we believe we are going to get a negative response. Anger, criticism, blame, defensiveness, pouting, resentment, and even silence is off-putting in a relationship. Your negative thoughts are like a dark cloud floating above your head; you may not see it, but others do. You must train your mind to focus on the affirmative side of life.

In addition to attracting others, positive thoughts allow you to see many more options in life. With a positive attitude you can see unlimited opportunities; choices just seem to appear. On the contrary, negative thinking most often leads to a dead-end street—and, many times, back to loneliness. You've probably tried to have a conversation with someone who is determined to be negative. With every suggestion, you get a "Yes, but . . ." or "I've tried that." It's so frustrating trying to cheer up someone who refuses your good intentions. By practicing right view, you will not be a source of frustration to others in this way. Here is an exercise to focus your thoughts and your feelings on right view.

Exercise 25: Right View Meditation

This meditation is an advanced strategy that assumes that you have completed the prior activities in this book. You will need to have a deep understanding that thoughts and memories are just thoughts and not facts; you can choose how you remember people and life events.

We invite you to use this exercise to focus your mind on positives. Remember, you have control of your mind and all of its thoughts. If negative information starts to creep in, just let it flow away from you like a leaf floating down a stream; bring your mind back to positive thoughts.

This meditation has several parts. Do as many as you have time for; any of them will produce a benefit. As you practice, you will begin to notice people who are being helpful in their daily lives by holding doors open, brewing and serving coffee, cleaning floors, and saying hello. It is through their kindness that we can all be well and happy.

Focus and relax in the way that is most comfortable for you.

Begin by thinking of your parents or your primary caregiver(s) when you were a child. As you focus on this point in your life, become aware of what your body was like when you were smaller and fragile and helpless. Think of the person who helped you the most. If a clear picture doesn't emerge, feel free to use your creativity and imagine what it must have been like. Imagine being dependent and vulnerable. Imagine being fed, bathed, helped on the toilet, and clothed. Picture all phases of your upbringing, from childhood through adolescence and adulthood. Think of all the ways your caregivers have been loving to you and how you could trust them to be in your corner. If a problematic picture arises, accept the fact that parents (or other adults) are human, too, and forgive them as you try to better understand just how difficult their job was. Then let the image flow away from you.

Focus on your feelings of gratitude for all the people who have enabled you to be where you are today. See the people who grow your food; hear the sounds of manufacturing as your shoes are made. Smell the fresh air that is produced when people plant trees and grow flowers. Taste the sweetness of safety that has been made possible by friends, neighbors, or law enforcement personnel who look out for you. Touch the fabric of your clothes that have been made by people you don't even know. See yourself repaying their kindness by being kind to them as well as to all others.

Move on to contemplate significant people in your upbringing: someone who noticed you, understood you, or took care of you. Think of other family members, teachers, and coaches. Thank them and feel the feelings of gratitude.

Move on to contemplate the kindness of the many others who work to provide you with the essentials of life. Think of the work that goes into each part of their jobs and how much labor it takes to provide for our daily sustenance. Think of the wheat that is grown for bread and all the workers it takes to harvest the wheat; then think of the bakers who baked the bread, the carriers who transported the bread, and the cashier whom you paid for the bread. Contemplate the kindness of all the people who make your life possible; thank them and wish that they be happy, peaceful, safe, and free. Finally, notice all of the people in your daily life who provide deliberate or random acts of kindness to others.

There are so many positive aspects to life; you will see them when you look for them. Being optimistic is a prerequisite for living life in the Middle Way.

The next two steps, right concentration and right mindfulness, will help you to continue to discipline your mind, feelings, and actions, regardless of the reality of life. This is powerful. You get to decide how your mind works and how lonely or never lonely you will be.

Right Concentration

The streets of McLeod Ganj (the section of Dharamsala closest to His Holiness's compound) are lined with vendors offering an array of goods. They have jewelry galore, shawls of every fabric, and an unlimited supply of Buddhist memorabilia. The variety makes for colorful photos and an endless temptation for shopping and bargaining.

Many vendors take a "something for everybody" approach to sales: If you are not in the market for pashmina (a type of wool like cashmere) or gemstones, then how about a Buddhist souvenir? As we made our way from shop to shop, we began to notice a pattern in the merchandise that was offered. A significant number of the items for sale seemed to fall under the category of what we Westerners might call concentration aids: devices and gadgets designed to focus attention and promote single-mindedness. There were bells, chimes, singing bowls, prayer wheels for the table, prayer wheels for the walls, prayer wheels on a stick—all to help you focus and concentrate.

Even someone who has never practiced meditation can be drawn in by the reverberating sound of small brass cymbals, called *tingsha*, being chimed together. The natural inclination is to pay attention, focus on the sound, and stay attuned until the sound waves dissipate. Concentrating on the sound makes it easier to focus and calm yourself; that's why these aids are so helpful. The singing bowl has a similar effect. Running a wooden pestle around the edge of a brass bowl produces a hum or a ringing noise that also captures and focuses your attention.

You don't have to use a device to concentrate and focus your mind, but those of us who have a lot of internal chatter, or monkey mind, find them helpful. As you read this book and put its suggestions into action, it's important to keep your mind focused on your core values, your connections to others, your community involvement, the use of your talents in meaningful work, and living out the purpose of your life in the Middle Way. If you do not concentrate on your thoughts, feelings, and actions, you can be pulled back into old habits that may lead to loneliness. Right concentration will keep you on track.

If you met us, it would not take you long to figure out which one of us is a natural with concentration. Jon is a man of few words, not because of shyness or a lack of interest (he's very present), but because his mind focuses on one thing at a time with practiced ease. Pat, in contrast, has a mind like a dram of mercury, prone to split into numerous droplets at the slightest nudge. Needless to say, learning to concentrate and be more focused has been a lifelong challenge for her.

"From an early age," Pat recalls, "I kept my mind moving in several directions at once. When caught in a situation that required concentration, like church, I'd sit in the pew and count the panes on the stained-glass windows, then the ceiling tiles, and then the people sitting in each row. My mind was so accustomed to racing around that slowing down or trying to focus felt like hitting a wall of anxiety. Over the years I tried various methods to bridle my racing mind. I took yoga, did breath work, tried chanting, took meditation classes, and went to silent retreats, but I still longed for the clear mind of 'om.' I was never successful until I read the teachings of the Dalai Lama. His reasonable practicality validated my frustration and then gave me a simple way to harness my wandering mind."

The Dalai Lama explained that monks and students practice meditation for years without experiencing moments of enlightened concentration. He said that most people make it far too complicated. Just sitting in a quiet place, noticing what is around you, is one way of concentrating. He was so encouraging and realistic, a living example of the Middle Way. He made the concept of right concentration accessible. He took away the mystery and made it manageable. Because of his practicality, Pat came up with her own concentration exercise, and it has truly changed her life. We predict that half of you will say, "So what's the big deal?" and the other half will say, "No, way, that's impossible." We challenge you to try it and let us know how it turns out for you.

Exercise 26: **Pat's Powerful Concentration Technique**

This technique is simple yet difficult. It has only one step: to simply do one thing at a time.

That's it. Whatever it is that you are doing, do it and nothing else. If you are reading this book, read this book. Focus on the words of the book; ignore the temptation to think about other things you could or should be doing, like checking your text messages, making yourself a snack, or changing your clothes. Just read the book. Once you finish reading, whatever you do next, do just that one thing. Concentrate, focus, and be single-minded. This doesn't mean that you shouldn't run the dishwasher and the washing machine at the same time; it means that you simply concentrate on one subject, person, task, feeling, or experience at a time.

This practice really did change Pat's life for the better. She, like many people, finds it especially difficult to concentrate in a single-minded fashion. Half of the smartest people in the world may be highly adept at multitasking, but multitasking can be a significant source of stress. We fall into the habit of multitasking because of the illusion that it is more efficient; in fact, the opposite is true. More mistakes are made when you are multitasking, more accidents occur, and multitasking is the number one cause of forgetfulness.

If none of those reasons convinces you to begin the practice of doing one thing at a time, consider this: you cannot be intimate when you are multitasking. You will not have those magic moments of connection, compassion, camaraderie, or communion with another when you are multitasking.

We all know how annoying and hurtful it is for someone to answer the phone while you are talking to him or her, or to be checking the e-mail while you are pouring your heart out. Multitasking creates a state of loneliness for all the people involved. The antidote is a simple form of concentration that can be practiced in the car, on the subway, while making love, or while changing a diaper: simply do one thing at a time.

The chances are that we have all experienced some form of right concentration. Jon notes, "Athletes often experience single-minded concentration when engrossed in their sport. We call it being in the 'groove' or the 'zone' or finding the 'sweet spot.' It happens when your body, your mind, and your energy are all focused on a single activity. I felt this 'runner's high' almost daily for years without realizing that this was available for all aspects of my life."

Knowing where your mind is at any given moment is a basic requirement for reinforcing the changes you make in your core values, your connections, your work, and your purpose in life. We encourage you to make the changes without going to extremes. Right concentration involves controlling your thoughts and your attention in a way that is conducive to life in the Middle Way.

Right Mindfulness

Right mindfulness addresses not only the focus of your mind but also the consequences of your behavior. We have already introduced you to the concept of mindfulness: being present in the moment and intentionally paying attention in a nonjudgmental way. Mindfulness is simply noticing what is happening without judging it. If you have been paying attention and practicing the exercises in this book, you should be more mindful by this point. If you haven't, then here's an opportunity to notice in a nonjudgmental way: "Hmm, I've read this whole book but haven't stopped to do the exercises." Or "Interesting that I haven't practiced being mindful."

Mindfulness means that you pay attention to your thoughts, your feelings, your behavior, and the consequences of each; then, once you notice them, you maintain an attitude of acceptance of what is. Instead of judging, you remain open. Once you notice your behavior, even if you slip into an old habit and judge yourself—"I should have been practicing mindfulness"—you have a chance to be curious, to be objective, and to change your internal dialogue: "Hmm, I'm being more mindful of my behavior right now." If your mind starts to judge or crave a different outcome, move it in the direction you want it to go. You get to choose.

Mindfulness gives you the opportunity to choose positive thoughts, feelings, and behavior, which in turn will make you happier and more content and will draw others to you. Mindfulness also increases your confidence; when you master the art of noticing your behavior and choosing how you respond, you can choose comfort in almost any situation. Mindfulness helps you to avoid extreme behaviors that create discomfort, and it enables you to make choices in line with the Middle Way.

As you increase your practice of mindfulness, you may realize that you have many thoughts in any given situation. You will discover that on some days your mind has more happy thoughts, whereas on other days you have more unhappy thoughts. Some thoughts, feelings, and actions are healthy and reinforce your core values, but others are negative and lead to distress. In some ways your mind is like a television: if you don't like what is playing on one channel, you can switch to another channel! You get to tailor your thoughts, feelings, and actions to fit your values and your purpose in life. Learning to watch thoughts, feelings, and behavior and to see them as they are and not as facts is a major component of right mindfulness. You get to choose how you think, feel, and act—that's a fact.

Practicing Mindfulness

Jon has his own way of practicing mindfulness that we introduced as the Tibetan Two-Step (Exercise 6). It simply involves breathing and being aware of your breathing. As simple as this exercise is (the only way to do it wrong is to not do it), it will increase your mindfulness by making you focus, concentrate, and be more aware of the present moment. The practice of mindfulness is not complicated, yet it is powerful because it gives you control of your thoughts, feelings, and behavior.

Some experts distinguish between a formal and an informal mindfulness practice. A formal practice means that you set aside a specific amount of time once or twice a day to devote to mindfulness exercises. The Tibetan Two-Step might fit this model.

An informal mindfulness practice takes place throughout the day; Pat's Powerful Concentration Technique (Exercise 26) might fit this model. You decide which is best for you. Think about your typical day and identify the activities: showering, dressing, eating, walking, driving, going to work, and so on. Each of these events can be a time for you to practice mindfulness by simply focusing on whatever you are doing at the moment. When your mind wanders into thoughts of the future or the past, gently return to the present and the task at hand. Being present and aware is the goal.

Here is a simple mindfulness exercise; let it serve as a reminder of the path of the Middle Way.

Exercise 27: **The Middle Way**

As you sit comfortably or as you walk, slowly repeat the following passage:

There is a Middle Way between self-indulgence and self-denial.

There is a Middle Way in which my thoughts, feelings, and behavior focus on the positive.

There is a Middle Way in which I am mindful and accepting.

There is a Middle Way free from sorrow and suffering.

There is a Middle Way in which there is no loneliness.

I walk in the Middle Way.

Right view, right concentration, and right mindfulness keep us in the Middle Way. It was by living in the Middle Way, as taught by the Dalai Lama, that we learned to never be lonely again. We will be forever grateful.

10

Never Be Lonely Again—
Your Choice

IF YOU WANT OTHERS TO BE HAPPY, PRACTICE COMPASSION.
IF YOU WANT TO BE HAPPY, PRACTICE COMPASSION.

—The Dalai Lama

As we write this last chapter, we have returned to Dharamsala for another audience with His Holiness the Dalai Lama. This time we are part of a larger group that calls itself the Old Dharamsala Wallahs (ODWs). It's a reunion of sorts, consisting of people who studied with His Holiness during the 1970s and 1980s; wallah, meaning a person involved in a certain type of activity. We were included in the group through an invitation by Jhampa to observe, record, and report our impressions of the conference. This fortuitous assignment fit right in with the completion of the book and provided a wonderful opportunity to retest our premises about loneliness with people from all over the world. We felt blessed by the privilege of hearing His Holiness speak for two consecutive days and of speaking with numerous people who have applied his principles to their lives. It was a fitting way to come full circle on our own path away from loneliness.

As the ODWs began to arrive in McLeod Ganj and move about town, many approached us to inquire if we were part of the group. As Westerners, we are pretty conspicuous in Dharamsala, and our ages place us in a demographic that could have been in India during the 1970s and 1980s. When asked directly if we were a part of the ODWs, we replied, "Well, sort of." After a brief explanation of our role, we got an opportunity to ask the questions we were anxious to explore, such as "What brought you to India many years ago?" and "Have you ever dealt with loneliness?" The answers we received were fascinating and far more validating than we had imagined they would be.

For example, we were quite surprised that in many of our interviews with the ODWs, the subject of loneliness came up before we ever mentioned it. This happened so often that it was a little disconcerting— almost as if the interviewees had been planted by the universe or we were telepathically communicating. We started every conversation the same way: "What brought you to India many years ago?" We found it quite interesting that many replied with some version of "I was lonely and came to find a home—not just a physical home, but an emotional, spiritual home."

When the two of us were comparing notes after our individual interviews, we were impressed with the uniqueness of the group and how un-Western it seemed to seek a solution for loneliness by going on a pilgrimage (90 percent of the ODWs were from the West: 20 percent from the United States and the rest from Europe and Australia). Today a Western approach to loneliness would far more likely include psychotherapy than a pilgrimage, treatment versus a trip. The ODWs were on to something, because if you chose treatment today, therapists without a thorough knowledge of loneliness might review your history, beginning with what was wrong with your family of origin and focusing on your disappointments and setbacks. But focusing on pathology or what was wrong with your upbringing is rarely the right approach for alleviating loneliness. A disappointing childhood or a history of failure can explain loneliness, but it inadvertently gives license to it.

We have found that moving away from loneliness requires being less distracted by one's own psychological history and processes and more focused on living in the present. Those in the ODW group who got it, who benefited the most from the pilgrimage, discovered that the path away from loneliness is far more other-focused than self-focused. Once you realize who you are and the core values you hold, then your attention appropriately turns to the quality of your close connections, how you relate to the broader community, how your talents are utilized in meaningful work, and how purposeful your life is. Caring for others, not just yourself, is the first step on the pilgrimage away from loneliness, whether you leave home or not.

The ODWs who found an antidote to loneliness in India didn't find it in the geographic location, nor did they find it in being close to the Dalai Lama. Those who returned without loneliness were those who had learned a new way of life. If you were to sum up this new lifestyle in one word, it would be *compassion*. Compassion simply means that you don't think and care only about yourself; you think and care about the welfare of others, and your actions prove it.

"It's a hard balance to strike," says Marc Ian Barasch, in his book *Field Notes on the Compassionate Life*. "If I am not for myself, who will be? But if I am only for myself, what am I?" he asks, quoting the first-century Jewish sage Hillel. "There is a growing sense in our society, left, right, and center, that the balance has woozily tipped; that our obsession with seamless self-contentment (What I love about Subway is it's all about me!) has occluded our ability to love and care about each other."

In the West, all too often our cultural default setting is to get our own needs met. Our psychosocial mean temperature, suggested by more than one recent article, is *people-friendly narcissism*, which means "be nice so you can get something you want for yourself."

If you think we're exaggerating about the narcissistic focus of Western culture, Google *self-empowerment*. You'll find that the resources go on and on. If you search for *other-empowerment*, you get a mixed bag, with many references leading back to self-empowerment. You don't see many seminars entitled Developing Compassion or Free Your Inner

Compassion. How many people are walking over hot coals to prove how kind or loving they are? It's always all about me.

The problem of self-focus has become so pronounced that we've had to examine our most basic assumptions about mental health. For decades the apex of adult maturity and adjustment has been measured by how autonomous you are. Recently, however, a group of (mostly female) psychologists has proposed openness to mutual influence— that is, the ability to collaborate with, commiserate with, consider, and be compassionate toward others as well as yourself—as a far more reliable barometer of mental health than the self-esteem of me-ness. The bottom line is this: whether you learn it in India or Indianapolis, the key to never being lonely again as well as to mature mental health is compassion, the simple act of caring for others as well as for yourself.

The very first morning in McLeod Ganj, Jon met a woman whose life choices exemplify caring for others.

"At five in the morning," he explains, "I was wandering the hotel corridor looking for Mohinder, the night manager, in order to get a cup of coffee. I was still in a jet-lag stupor and was somewhat startled when a door opened and, instead of Mohinder, out came a delightful woman named Nancy who was also on a Mohinder coffee search. We introduced ourselves as we shuffled down the hall to the kitchen, where Mohinder, who had already anticipated our need, was busy heating water on the gas stove. Since it takes awhile to bring water to a boil at six thousand feet, Nancy and I began to chat.

"She related a short personal history, including the fact that she is from New York but lives in India for several months each year in order to volunteer at the Tibetan Children's Village. She is retired, very young and radiant-looking at sixty-something, and spends eighteen hours a day working with the children at TCV. Each morning in India, she wakes at five o'clock in the morning, goes to the village to work, comes back to the hotel at night to sleep, then gets up the next morning and does it all again. I asked her how she could keep up the pace; she just smiled—beamed, actually—and said that now that she is retired, she spends all of her time in giving, and it is through giving that she has found her purpose in life."

We like to think that there are millions of people like Nancy who quietly go about lives of giving. We don't know how Nancy found her path; who knows, it might have even been through an empowerment seminar. What we discovered in our interviews with Nancy, the ODWs, and so many others was that caring for others creates a life of meaning—and when your life has meaning, there's no room for loneliness.

Who Am I in India?

As we continued to ask the question "What brought you to India many years ago?" loneliness was not the only answer we received. Much to our surprise and delight, a significant number of the ODW group came to Dharamsala in their twenties or thirties in search of an answer to "Who am I?" It was affirming to meet so many people who had traveled around the world with this question in mind. When you think about it, it makes sense. Going on a pilgrimage does provide the time and the space to examine your life as well as your core values.

Being away from familiar contexts can bring out parts of your personality that would otherwise remain hidden by the routine of everyday life. Predictable days full of busywork leave little time for reverie or reflection. You may have heard it said that work expands to fill the time you have to complete it. Thus, if you don't plan time for contemplation, there will always be more work to fill your time. Technically, we all have the same amount of time—twenty-four hours a day, seven days a week—so it's simply a matter of choice in how we use it. Nevertheless, being away from daily commitments can allow more time to ponder and reflect.

Our hope is that this book has provided a way for you to get away from your daily routine in order to determine your answers to "Who

Am I?" Reading this book may not equal taking a trip to India or studying in residence with the Dalai Lama, but each of us has a different path. Only you know what path you need to take. You might need to make your own pilgrimage of sorts, which could be as simple as a day of silent contemplation or a week away from your normal routine; perhaps it's a journey to a place of inspiration or even a retreat where leaders offer guidance.

We do know that the question "Who Am I?" is important enough to make some people travel around the world and create a totally different life, but it doesn't have to be that drastic. Of the 266 ODWs, only about 10 percent stayed ten years or more. Most stayed for far less time. Jhampa stayed in Dharamsala for fourteen years, and three and a half of those years were spent sitting in silence in a cave, but he was only one of about ten people who did this. Rob, Jhampa's "cave mate" who also spent three years in silence, explained to us, "The experience in Dharamsala was invaluable, but there comes a time when you want to have sex and a beer, so I went back to real life."

You don't have to turn your life upside down to discover who you are or have a different life. You simply have to make choices that lead away from loneliness.

From Loss to a Life of Meaning

Several of the people we interviewed said that they came to India to find more meaning in life. More than one person said that they just felt called, as though they were meant to come. But the third most frequent answer we heard when we asked "What brought you to India many years ago?" was to find solace after the loss of an important relationship or connection. Several people had lost more than one family member; others had lost a spouse. Two women came after they experienced a breach with their religious community. Another man came after a major career loss.

As we heard story after story that began with suffering but ended in a more compassionate life, we were reminded of the story of Siddhartha

Gautama, the Buddha. As we noted earlier, Suddhodana, Siddhartha's father, feared that if his son ever encountered suffering, sickness, or death, he would be filled with compassion and compelled to fulfill his destiny as a spiritual teacher rather than as an emperor—and Suddhodana's fears were well-founded. When Siddhartha saw the suffering of life and the losses that people had endured, he could no longer be content with his life of luxury. Hedonistic pleasures no longer satisfied him; beautiful surroundings didn't impress him. The suffering he experienced, as well as the suffering of others, activated his compassion and sent him on a pilgrimage to find an end to suffering.

So many of the people we talked to in Dharamsala had followed the trail of Siddhartha. After suffering loss or watching loved ones suffer, they left the comforts of home to seek a different life high in the foothills of the Himalayas. Did they all get what they came for? Some did, for sure; the rest, it's hard to say. One of the more humorous moments at the conference happened while the Dalai Lama was reflecting on the history of his former students who were there to honor him. He acknowledged that "many of you came for serious study, but others were just hippies whose minds went first this way and then that way!" That created laughter throughout the room, but several people later admitted that he had been quite accurate.

Which Way Does Your Mind Go?

With his humorous gibe, the Dalai Lama made an important point that can be applied to loneliness: you have to be in charge of your mind, or it will wander first this way and that way and ultimately end up back in the land of loneliness. If you have lived with loneliness for a period, you have probably spent a significant amount of time thinking about it.

Perhaps you have a movie in your head that reinforces the image of yourself as lonely. Your movie may even have a script that goes with it. Pat's script was "No one knows me, and no one wants to know me." Your script may be similar or different. You may even have musical accompaniment—a score, so to speak (think "Eleanor Rigby" by the Beatles)—and perhaps your own director style. Your movie may look like a Woody Allen screenplay or an even darker Alan Ball. What about Ingmar Bergman—could he have written the loneliness script in your head? Regardless, the thoughts you revisit over and over are simply a projection, just like in the movies.

Wes Nisker, in his book *Buddha's Nature: A Practical Guide to Discovering Your Place in the Cosmos*, has a provocative commentary on this subject, using the analogy of watching a movie:

> When we are watching the screen, we are absorbed in the momentum of the story, our thoughts and emotions manipulated by the images we are seeing. But if just for a moment we were to turn around and look toward the back of the theater at the projector, we would see how these images are being produced. We would recognize that what we are lost in is nothing more than flickering beams of light. Although we might be able to turn back and lose ourselves once again in the movie, its power over us would be diminished. The illusion maker has been seen.

Your mind is an illusion maker. You are able to choose your thoughts and your feelings. You can choose to move your thoughts, your feelings, and ultimately your actions away from the images of loneliness. Following the exercises and prescriptions in this book will help you to write your own screenplay; it's your choice. With this in mind, we offer you one final exercise, designed to move you from suffering and loneliness to a life of compassion.

Exercise 28: **Creating Compassion**

The most common meditation for creating compassion involves understanding your own suffering as well as the suffering of others and the wish to be free of it.

Focus and relax. Visualize your desire to be happy, safe, peaceful, and free. Continue by acknowledging that all people long to be happy, safe, peaceful, and free.

Let your mind begin to explore the suffering you have experienced, the loneliness you have felt, the hurt you have endured, the disabilities and challenges that plague your life. Think of emotional pain, physical pain, and financial hardships that you have lived with. Now express the desire to be free of all suffering and pain. Repeat, "May I be free of suffering" and "May I be free of pain."

When you feel comfortable, move on to compassion by getting a clear image of someone else who is suffering. Imagine what suffering might be like for this person, then express the desire that he or she be free of all pain and suffering.

Now get a clear image of someone who is lonely. Imagine what the loneliness is like; then express the desire that he or she be free of loneliness: "May he or she be free of loneliness."

Move on to offering compassion to friends who are suffering and others you know. Express the desire that they be free of suffering: "May they be free of suffering." Imagine them being happy, safe, peaceful, and free.

Finally, think of those who are your enemies or those who trouble you. Understand that they are suffering and that you desire that they, too, be free of pain and suffering: "May they be free of suffering." Imagine them being happy, safe, peaceful, and free.

When you are ready and so inclined, express the desire that all beings be happy, safe, peaceful, and free. Understand that no one likes pain and suffering. Focus on all the problems in the world: poverty, war, famine, hunger, job loss, physical injury, disease, violence, and so on. Understand that all living beings have a right to life and happiness. Imagine the world as happy, safe, peaceful, and free.

The heart of compassion is the ability to put ourselves in another's shoes. You can deepen your experience of compassion by taking time each day to acknowledge that all beings want to be happy, safe, peaceful, and free—just as you do. Imprint your mind with this truth. When you find yourself becoming stressed, frustrated, or intolerant, think of how all people are doing the best they can to find happiness. Focus on being thoughtful and considerate when you feel yourself getting angry; remind yourself that everyone wants to be free from suffering. Creating compassion every day through this exercise will increase your level of empathy and shift your focus away from loneliness. It's simple yet powerful.

Who Gets Lonely?

As you finish this book and continue on your journey away from loneliness, it might be helpful to remind yourself how far you've come as well as how to get back on track if you find loneliness creeping back into your life. A person who gets lonely is usually experiencing one or more of the following:

1. Being out of sync with his or her core values
2. Being without ongoing connection with other people
3. Having little or no interest in furthering the welfare of others
4. Having no meaningful work
5. Not following one's life purpose

It is heartening to remember that you can turn away from loneliness at any given moment by simply focusing on these issues.

If you know what it is like to be lonely, then you know what it is like to suffer. The question then is how you will choose to respond to the suffering. Our deepest pain and our strongest feelings of loss are designed to bring us back to our better selves. For each of us, this is the self that practices loving-kindness, the self that has known suffering and that therefore has the desire to end suffering in others, and the self that lives a life of compassion.

"If you want others to be happy, practice compassion. If you want to be happy, practice compassion." If you follow this simple advice from the Dalai Lama, you will never be lonely again.

Jon Carlson, His Holiness the Dalai Lama, and Pat Love

Index

About the Authors

Pat Love, Ed.D., is a distinguished professor, author, trainer, and long-standing licensed clinician. For thirty years, she has contributed to counselor education and personal development through her books, articles, training programs, speaking and media appearances. Dr. Love has published several professional articles, has been featured in several professional books, and has developed relationship education media and materials for national and international use. Her ever-popular books *Hot Monogamy* and *The Truth About Love* have taken her around the world spreading the good news about family and relationships. Her latest book, *How to Improve Your Relationship Without Talking About It*, has been translated into twelve languages. Dr. Love is in demand as an expert presenter at national and international conferences. She has appeared numerous times on *Oprah*, the *Today* show, and CNN, and is a regular contributor to popular magazines, including *Psychology Today*. Dr. Love has cohosted three DVD training programs: *Living Love, Parenting with the Experts,* and *Love: Everything You Need to Know*—which is currently available on PBS. Visit her at www.patlove.com.

Jon Carlson, Psy.D., Ed.D., ABPP, is a distinguished professor of psychology and counseling at Governors State University and a psychologist at the Wellness Clinic in Lake Geneva, Wisconsin. Dr. Carlson has served as editor of several periodicals including the *Journal of Individual Psychology* and *The Family Journal.* He holds diplomates in both family psychology and Adlerian psychology. He has authored 150 journal articles and fifty books including *Time for a Better Marriage, Adlerian Therapy, Inclusive Cultural Empathy, The Mummy at the Dining Room Table, Bad Therapy, The Client Who Changed Me, Their Finest Hour, Creative Breakthroughs in Therapy,* and *Moved by the Spirit.* He has created more than 250 professional trade video and DVDs with leading professional therapists and educators. In 2004 the American Counseling Association named him a "Living Legend." In 2009 the Division of Psychotherapy of the American Psychological Association named him "Distinguished Psychologist" for his life contribution to psychotherapy. He has received similar awards from four other professional organizations. He recently syndicated the advice cartoon *On The Edge* with cartoonist Joe Martin. Dr. Carlson has been married to his wife Laura for forty-two years. They have five children. Visit him at www.joncarlson.org.